TRANSITIONS

DEATH PROCESSES & BEYOND OF 11 ENTITIES

BOOK 13

VERLING CHAKO PRIEST, PH.D.

Order this book online at www.trafford.com
or email orders@trafford.com

Most Trafford titles are also available at major online book retailers.

Print information available on the last page.

ISBN: 978-1-4907-5836-7 (sc)
ISBN: 978-1-4907-5838-1 (hc)
ISBN: 978-1-4907-5837-4 (e)

Library of Congress Control Number: 2015905668

Trafford rev. 04/13/2015

 www.trafford.com

North America & international
toll-free: 1 888 232 4444 (USA & Canada)
fax: 812 355 4082

CONTENTS

DEDICATION

I dedicate Book 13 to the 11 Entities who came to me so sincerely to tell the readers about their death stories. May God bless them as they reincarnate back to Earth.

FOREWORD

It has been a long time since I have been this excited about bringing in a new book. I awake in the morning and lie in bed planning the book. Jeshua is my gate keeper, so I have left it up to him as to when the beginning date will be. He has now told me it will be Tuesday, February 24, 2015.

Anonymity is my main concern, not only for the privacy of any living relatives but also for all the legalese that could ensue if a relative takes offense in any way. I have thought of naming the deceased people who come forth to share their death-story using a 001, 002, 003, but then I remembered there is a 007 named James Bond. I would have to delete that number. However, after much thought, I decided to just skip that whole way of identifying the Entities.

As I continued ruminating on my book, I wanted a cross section of people who were similar to the nursery rhyme: *rich-man, poor-man, beggar-man, thief, doctor, lawyer, merchant, chief, clergyman, military-man, and Ascended Master.* I also wanted different illnesses or acts of violence. Many people were dying from Multiple Sclerosis (MS). There were those who died of the Plague years ago. And I did not want to ignore those who had chosen a life of violence, the gun slingers in the Wild West, and died from the bullets that pelted their bodies. As to whether the participants are Masters or not and it is one of their past lives, we will never know. Remember, *anonymity*. And are there even those people available from the Wild West, or have they reincarnated by now?

I spoke with Jeshua/Sananda today. We set the date for the launching of my new book: **Tuesday, 02-24-15**. I am so delighted. 02-07-15.

It will be a great adventure for us all—the Entities who participate, for me, the author, and for you readers.

Read on!

INTRODUCTION

O2-24-15 Precious one, I am Sananda and I have come this morning (6:55 AM) for we are going to launch your Book 13. We too are feeling great joy. This will be a different project for you. To put you at ease, your space is well protected. There is a ring-pass-not so as we bring the Beings forth, we also see to it that they leave. Thanks; they know the procedure? *Yes, they have been well drilled, shall we say. They too are excited. It is not often they get to tell their story to the world, so they are really looking forward to this. So let me get to the INTRODUCTIION, dear one and we can take it from there.* And may I ask you questions afterwards? *Yes, by all means. (*Sananda continues.*)*

We have asked Chako, our beautiful scribe, to channel a book that is somewhat different than she is used to. We will be bringing to her incarnate Entities who wish to tell their story. There are so many untruths in the bible concerning the pearly gates and St. Peter and streets of gold as one enters Heaven. We wish to tell truth here and let the Beings themselves say what their experience was.

Everyone just thinks they go to Heaven. Where is Heaven? Heaven is like another planet. I will not go into this for others have described it. We do not wish to plagiarize in any way. I refer you to *Matthew's Messages* by Suzy Ward. (*See the 02-08-15 issue*).

So they get to Heaven (or *Nirvana*, as Matthew calls it) and they are usually astounded because of the great love they encounter. One of the first goals of the Angels as they greet them is to help erase the fears that they will be punished. Imagine their surprise when all that they encounter is *love*. They soon forget what all their belief systems were. They exclaim as to why did not someone tell them it was like this? And of course those in *New Age Thought* already know how it is in what is called *Heaven—a place of love*.

The Entities *cry how can this be? It is more beautiful than anything I experienced in my lifetime. It is easy to move around. I only have to think something and it happens. If I want to go for a train ride, suddenly I am at a train station. I can hop on. I and the other passengers take rides through beautiful mountains. Or if one is into flying, all of a sudden the Being is at an airport and is flying in a plane.* Many Beings have never been in an airplane before. They were always afraid it was going to crash. And of course there are no plane crashes in Heaven. Some have never taken a helicopter ride so they are given that choice.

Some people are always in the kitchens, loving the culinary fare—fine dining. They have only to think of that when lo and behold they are there and they are being taught how to make these delicious dishes that they had only read about in that past life, which they no longer think of as *home*. Heaven is now Home to them—God's world.

Many wonder and are afraid because they had always heard that you go and stand in front of God and have the Judgment Day. And of course that is all erroneous also. God does look in upon the new arrivals but he does not always appear as the new arrivals expect him to be. He is not seated on his throne, but he can walk among them in his glory if he chooses. It is very simple. You just create a hologram that looks like a body.

Some of the Entities have never been to the seashore, played in the sand, made sand castles. This is especially true of children who have just passed over. There is no fear that they might drown. One might say, you are already dead so why worry about dying! (*Chuckles*). They find that they cannot sink; there is always sand beneath their feet. The dolphins come and play with them. If it sounds like a fantasy fairy land; it is! Anything you imagine is immediately before you.

We will not get into the darker adventure where Entities are in their dark side and think there is a Hell. They are merely creating their dark thoughts of being in jail, etcetera. There is no punishment, fire and brimstone. Those are all beliefs that will be lovingly released by the Angels.

There are Entities who are attached to beautiful bodies, so they are given a form to reside in, one that they will recognize for when they were around thirty and healthy. However, it is not necessary. They could have a body that looks like they did at 60 years of age. You see it is whatever is in the heart. That is what is manifested for them.

To get back to the culinary department, they are taught to make delicious dishes. They can eat them and really enjoy their culinary efforts. Now it is true, animals are not killed for food. It is not necessary. The food there that they are instructed to prepare would make Vegans very happy. It is so fresh and crisp—no animal meat.

After a while the Beings may realize they have missed a meal. *Oh my gosh, I missed lunch call. I forgot all about lunch.* You see they were not hungry. They do not have to have food, so gradually they give up the food idea. But I am afraid those in the culinary kitchens still keep food as their focus.

Yes, we have what Chako calls the *hospital-in-the-sky*. Only they are *Care Centers*. When people cross over, their bodies can be so ravaged by cancer or wars—lost limbs and so forth. They are taken to different areas and they are repaired. They are put into a beautiful sleep and with Light, sounds, and crystals their bodies are made whole again. Gradually, they are awakened. They realize that they do not remember much of when they were ill. They do marvel at the fact that they can walk again. So they walk and dance—all the things they were not able to do when they had a debilitating disease, perhaps like Multiple Sclerosis (MS).

Then there are those Beings who were into sports—what was referred to as *sports-stars*—who cross over. Many of the football players who eventually die are surprised to find just how injured their brain was by playing that game. As they have their review, they realize that the tremendous monies that were paid to them in their contracts had reach the point of being ridiculous. They saw how they had squandered it on—a man's toys—the beautiful cars that were collected, then just sitting around, not being put to use. But they are the collectibles to the wealthy minded. It is not only the sports people, but others. You do not find too many women collecting cars. She likes a luxurious car, but she is not that enamored in finding an antique to restore. Then the owners are afraid to drive the car for fear it will get dirty or you will pop a tire. (*Remember, old vintage cars had balloon tires on them with an inner tube.*)

Therefore, the Entities who cross over, these over-paid sports-people begin to see how much of their energy was wasted on possessions. They start to realize how they could have done so much more with that money. They look at the jewels they wore—the heavy gold chains, the huge rings—all for show. As they start to see, they say to themselves, *what's wrong with this picture?*

Now in Heaven they can have all of that, ten times over if they wish. They can have so many gold chains on themselves they can barely raise their shoulders. *But why,* they start to say to themselves—*but why?* Now there is an energy in gold that can be healing. However, it is like anything else, too much of a good thing and it is over-kill.

Let's see what else. Oh yes, the sportsmen, the hunters who like to go out and hunt and kill big game. Now they can see all those animals that they had killed in that lifetime. They see them roaming freely, not harming anyone. You can go up to them and pet them. They then get a mental picture of a polar bear or a tiger or a beautiful stag-deer with massive antlers that they had killed and had hung on their wall.

You see one of the things, while everyone is enjoying all that Heaven has to offer, what they do not realize is that they are gradually being retrained. They begin to feel what truth is and what truth is not. They become educated; they start to communicate with the animals. They are taught that their thoughts will manifest. They are surprised to learn telepathy.

Many of the Entities who will be coming to this channel will be doing something they had never done before in that lifetime. They pooh-poohed it; thought it was nuts that somebody could speak to and hear the thoughts of a dead person.

Many books are written and not even read by family members for they believed that the books were the fantasy of that author, whether a family relative or not. They did not believe the truth that was being written out for them. Now Beings from all walks of life are learning while in Heaven about their lost opportunity—not only to learn valuable information, but to elevate their relative to a position of respect.

I think one of the most painful lessons while on Earth is the loss of a loved one—human or pet—and all of the erroneous belief systems surrounding that. Now they are finding out just how much the heart is involved. They learn and recognize their own levels of love. Did they use love as possessing, as sex, as control? Did they really appreciate their partner? Did they receive the love that was given to them from others?

They were experiencing in Heaven what true love is. They only had to be around the Angels. Sometimes the Angels appeared like fiction has stated—dressed in all white with their huge wings. That is all kind of a formal dress that is used only on special occasions. That is not necessary. Most of the Angels walk around just like, we'll say the dead people do (*chuckles*) and the Entities would be drawn to them. They would squat on the grass to hear their teachings from these wise Angels.

There was always much excitement when a great Ascended Master came to visit. My Jesus part was called upon frequently for that was all people knew. *Oh Jesus save me.* Now they are finding out that Jesus did not save anyone. It was their soul who saved them. But interestingly enough these Entities in their Earth life did not always believe that they had a soul. And if they could acknowledge that, they did not know what to do about that. It never occurred to them to communicate with their soul. Most people were just coming from their ego—climbing on the shoulders of anyone to advance their cause.

Those who are reading this book turn to the Appendix and read the article we wrote on *God's Children* for his Book 7. It will be self-explanatory if you wish to learn more about what God calls *The Seasons of the Soul.*

Now let's see. Oh yes, the dear Evangelists—those zealous preachers who thought they had the voice of Jesus. *This is what he said and meant.* I find it interesting that all of them asked for money. They always coached it in terms that would draw people to them and give to their cause. There were those that did do good works, but they were not always correct in what they said. Now they are learning the truth about me and my Jesus-part. The various Entities have their review and what is known now as their past life. My Jesus life contained many painful moments. So the religious fanatics learn truth.

There is an interesting phenomenon that happens in Heaven. There is so much truth that they cannot handle it. They scramble to sign up again, to reincarnate again, to get back into their body again and start over. *Oh I can do it this time; I know what I did wrong last time; I can do it this time.* They had not stayed in Heaven that long in order to retrain themselves. And so their Master guide and Angels let them go back for another Earth life. All of them sign a contract that they will love deeply the Earth planet they revisit. Gaia does not need more people coming to destroy her. She too is ascending and needs only those who will help uplift her and treat her kindly and be appreciative of all the beautiful animals and vegetation that she provides.

There are all levels in Heaven, dear readers. You do not just pop into Heaven and think of it as just one grand school reunion and then go back to Earth to your old ways. No, there are all levels. Each level is earned by that soul. Some souls take a long time to learn their lessons and must repeat their lifetimes, but it is always their choice. No one makes them do anything. These are always the choices by the soul.

Now you will find as you read the book, that Chako has asked us to bring forth souls who had lifetimes in different categories. In order to do that, she chose the nursery rhyme of: Rich-man, Poor-man. Beggar-man, Thief-man, Doctor-man, Lawyer-man, Merchant-man, Chief-man, Clergy-man, Military-man, and the eleventh Entity, Ascended-man. There will be 11 Entities and 11 journeys. We hope by the end of the book, you will have a more clear idea of what Heaven is like. Its purpose is to give the souls solace—a respite after difficult lifetimes— to retrain them and help them know truth, to know love and have that grow so that each time they reincarnate they can come back at a deeper level of love for humanity.

I Am Sananda and we hope you enjoy what we have created for you. It will be a glorious book and we are all looking forward to it. Read on dear readers; read on!

1 RICH-MAN

0 2-27-15 Friday, 7:50 AM.

Good morning, precious one; all ready to bring in your first chapter?
Yes, I am.

I am Sananda. The Being who will be coming forth bears the code of
Rich-man. He has been told not to speak any names because of legal issues
that could arise from people who knew him, or from relatives of the past.
Anonymity must be kept at all times. He will be able to speak as long as
you wish without his energy fading out. So I will step back and let him
come forward. Thank you.

Good morning; I am very honored to be allowed into your force-field
in order to bring you descriptions of my death. *Thank you and greetings*
to you. You have been told that your code name will be Rich-man, *simply*
because we are using the nursery rhyme depicting the different categories
souls may use for their life's lessons.

That is fine with me. I wish to back up a bit and say that my body was
ravaged with the disease that is called *multiple sclerosis (MS)*. I was
totally incapacitated. But I was fortunate in the fact that I had the
funds to hire the best help and could easily afford it.

When the time came for my passing, I was in hospice care. I had not eaten for a couple of days. My body felt so tired and I was cold. I had relatives around me, and I was allowed to say goodbye to my favorite pet—a beautiful little dog who liked to cuddle with me. So they brought her in and we had our last cuddle. Then they took her away for sanitation purposes.

I laid there and thought of many things over my lifetime. I was not all that old—65 years old. But I had had a full life. I had traveled a great deal. I thought of all my different journeys; I thought of my family. I thought of those people I liked and did not like. When one is in the business world, one meets a myriad of people.

So I lay there and kind of just dozed, thinking of my many years' experiences. I was not into the metaphysical world, so I did not know all those terms that you know. Then I just kind of slipped out of my body. In fact it rather astonished me because one minute I am lying in my bed and the next I am out of bed and standing looking down at my body that is still in bed! I also observed all the people who had gathered around me moaning, crying, and grieving.

I did not stay there very long. You may find this unusual, but I still carried my emotions. You see, I knew I was going to die; then I knew that I was dead. And then to have all these people crying… It was depressing. I wanted to just leave. And of course, as soon as I thought that, it happened.

The next thing I knew I was sort of zooming off—similar, I suppose, to a rocket ship, except there was no ship! All of a sudden you are just moving at a tremendous speed. I saw no tunnel. There was no darkness. There was just… I don't even have the word to explain it. It was like I was floating up in the sky, except I wasn't floating; I was traveling at a tremendous speed.

The next thing I noted was there were Angels by my side. I heard: *You can stand up now.* And of course this was the first time I had been able to stand up by myself for years because of my MS disease. So I stood up and was absolutely delighted that I was able to move again. I started walking and then just to see if I could, I started running and flapping my arms, almost like a child does. I was in such joy.

The Angels caught up with me and exclaimed, *whoa, slow down, good sir; slow down.* I replied, *where am I?* They said, *don't you know?* I replied, *I am not sure. The Bible says when you are in Heaven, there are pearly gates and St. Peter. Are any of you St. Peter?* They sort of smiled and said, *no, we are Angels.* So I said, *where are the pearly gates and all of that?* They then said, *in your imagination. What you think you will see.*

So I said to myself, *all right let's see some pearly gates!* And lo and behold, I was standing in front of some pearly gates. They were very beautiful and just enormous. I said to the Angels who were still with me, *are these real?* They said, *well you just manifested them from your thoughts, so they are real; but you can just kind of dissolve them too, if you wish.* I replied, *why would I want to do that?* They answered, *because they are not needed. This is just a belief that has manifested because of your thought.* I replied, *oh, OK, I will just believe and un-manifest them.* And the gates just disappeared.

The Angels slowly guided me into what is called Heaven. There are beautiful buildings. I did not know which one to go to first. An Angel said, *why don't we go to the Care Center, for there are still parts of your body that need to be healed.*

You see, in order to return to another life... Do you believe in reincarnation? I replied, *well, I guess I do, but I am not sure.* They said, *well, you will be retrained. We assure you that when you leave, you will* *believe in reincarnation. Anyway, as we were saying... * They just talked to me like a next door neighbor.

Your dead body is still lying there in the hospice bed and will be taken to the mortuary and be cremated per your wishes. But you are in what we call your etheric body, and it is an exact replica of the body you had. But you still carry in your memory banks the pictures from the cells of your former body. Those cells are ill, so you will need to undergo a time where you will be peacefully asleep so that the healers can heal your body. We do it with crystals, different sounds, and Lights. It is a very pleasing experience, and you will come out feeling even better than you do now.

Therefore, they led me to this awesome building; it was huge. But strangely, it had no ceiling to it—no top. There was an entrance. The building had different floors, I guess you would call them—and you would step into an elevator and be whisked up to a certain floor. At that level there were other Angels who greeted you. They wore different colors. They did not flap around in their wings. They wore colored robes simply because they were more comfortable to wear, whether man, woman, or Angel. You did not have to wear a dress, or you did not have to wear trousers. You wore just a simple robe of pleasing colors. Some of the healers wore jewels because they held a certain energy that healed. Some wore gold rings or necklaces and used the properties from them to heal.

There were just beautiful crystals—huge amethysts—standing on the floor, all emitting healing energies—huge, huge stones. I remembered being taken to my little section. I laid down and these soothing sounds like music started wafting over me. I just fell into a deep sleep. I felt no fear. Actually, I was never afraid during the whole experience. It was all so new to me. Earth people who are into metaphysics know all about healings like this. But to me it was all so new and so strange. I just loved it! I remember in my Earth life when I traveled, I loved seeing all the different places.

In my business, I was bringing different communication systems to them—telephones and things of that nature. However, that is all starting to fade, and I now do not think about it all that much. So in the Caring Center, I fell into this deep sleep. When I woke up, it was just like awakening back home. I felt much rested and knew I had had dreams, but I did not pay that much attention to them. Therefore, I just sat up and found that I too had on a robe. It was kind of a dusky blue. Of course as you know, men were not allowed to wear many colors, at least not in my day. The only time that I could wear a dusky blue color would be in a shirt.

Then the next thing that I knew, the Angels, who were still with me, led me to another building—again a building with no ceilings. I found that strange, but I accepted it so did not even think to ask, *how come?* I noted that when one is in Heaven and sees all these things that are strange, and at the same time accepted, that one simply does not ask about them. It is just the way of things.

They led me then to this other building. It was a building I was more familiar with, although I had never seen it before. It had all computers and things of that nature inside. I got excited until I found out what it was. It is where the soul sees, hears, and feels the review of his departed lifetime.

I thought, *oh, no! I am going to fail that one.* I was not always a very nice person, you see. I was very strict and disciplined my employees severely and fired people easily. As I sat down in front of this huge computer screen and my review started, I started feeling every picture I saw. It went clear back to when I was a baby and how my parents treated me! Then I saw me as a toddler and what was it like when

I could not walk very well and people kind of laughed at me and thought it was funny. I was trying so hard to walk and I couldn't understand why people laughed at me.

The next thing I saw were school scenes and how my personality was molded. My family members were not, as one would say now, of the heart. I knew that they loved me, but they were stern. There was fighting among the siblings. No one had much respect for each other. What we respected was the discipline. Therefore, I saw in my review how that was carried over. I felt the same anger that I had as a ten year old. It was like I was there all over again. I felt everything. I saw when I was really mad and was cursing inappropriately, using words I would not dare in front of my father. I saw all of that again, experienced all of that; experienced the anger; experienced the guilt for the words I had spoken.

Then I went further along in that lifetime, and I saw how my emotions were changing. I saw when I had met my first love and how much it had affected me and how afraid I was. I was so afraid that I would say or do something that would make her upset and not like me that I was tongue-tied. It was almost like I was with her, but visiting her from afar and not able to speak much. That was my first love and then it went on and on and on. I had several loves in my life and many women.

Therefore, while the review in one way was not as frightening as I thought it would be—I did not appear before God and get damned and anything else he might do—I did feel all the negative actions that I had done; I actually felt them. Oh how I wished I could go back and change all of that. I felt how lacking love was in my heart. I did not love all that deeply. I was so into my ego—you know, a man's world, being a CEO, being an owner; controlling all of these people; into power. Then in my review it was not all that wonderful, for I felt both sides of the coin. I felt all my power and ego, but then I felt the recipients' emotions. Sometimes they were angry or guilty with me; they hated me. Or they just gave up their autonomy and let me control them. So I was so happy when my Angel guides said, *OK, it is time to go*. I had reached in my review the final end to that life—laying in the hospice bed with my dear wife sobbing over me.

The Angel guides are very good to the newcomers into Heaven. They knew we had just gone through a tremendous review and that we were experiencing the ups and downs and feeling very dejected and not in a good place. Therefore, the next thing they would do is let the people have their thoughts but there was uh—almost like a counseling session. You were not by yourself but with a group. I went into this room and all of a sudden here were all these people. Everyone else seemed to have the same problems of guilt and anger. I guess one could call this an *Anger Management* class, or something like that. We all just started talking how we felt about our review.

The Angel Facilitator started what I now know was to retrain us, to tell us why we did something and that how that needs to change. In other words, they were changing our erroneous belief systems. It was understood that we would be attending these sessions for as long as we resided there. It is interesting to note, I now know what that saying, *as above, so below*, means. The souls tend to have periods that they kind of re-enact times in life—like group therapy. We did that.

There were no days and nights. There was no *time* as we knew it on Earth, we soon learned. We soon forgot Earth-time. Pretty soon we started meeting loved ones who had already passed over. Now since I was in my sixties, I had never met many of the people in my family tree. Therefore, it was interesting to speak with them and compare experiences. I cannot say that I had a particular loved one that I met here. They were just all relatives and friends—golf partners at one time or another. So we did that.

Now you may be wanting to know what about religions? There are no religions in Heaven. We just knew there was a God watching over us, but we never saw Him. I never went to the Judgment Seat. It seems as if the Angels just guided us hither and yon. Then pretty soon they gave us more leeway. We learned that anything we thought about would just happen. Of course there was always an Angel guide when we felt like we needed one.

It is like you are watched over. It is not like you will get into trouble; it is just that you are watched over with such love, so that you are always experiencing love. I think that is the part I wish to talk about the most. We are always experiencing love.

Every once in a while, a great excitement would happen throughout the community. I learned it was because a great Being, an Ascended Master or someone like that, would be coming to visit. Of course everyone wanted to see Jesus because that was the only one we knew, or I should say, I knew, because I was not in a different belief system while I was on Earth.

Now I must say he filled everyone's expectations. He was glorious. He was in his robes, and you could see the colors that were coming out from all that surrounded him. When you came within that radius of his Light, you felt the peace and you felt his love. It was almost overwhelming and you wanted to follow him. But he had a way of letting you come just so close and then he smiled and kind of floated away as we all stood there and watched, not realizing that his energy alone had given us a magnificent healing.

I was so excited when he came to me, we'll say years later, and asked if I would be willing to be one of the people who would tell my death story for this book that you are writing. I was so excited. He explained that there could be a section in the book that you are calling Q & A—Questions & Answers. So I am open to anything you wish to ask me.

Thank you, Rich-man, and I am using your code name. Yes, and it is quite alright. *I thank you for being open to my asking you questions. They are just simple little questions that I will ask you.*

Questions (Q) and Answers (A)

You have already answered one of them. (How old were you when you died? And you said, 65.)

Q: *How long has it been since you have had a body?*

A: It has been many years and I do not know the exact number, but it has been many.

Q: *What form do you have now?*

A: I dropped that etheric body eons ago and I am now in a free spirit form.*

Q: *And in that life time, what was your purpose?*

A: Ah, that was a hard one for me. I still remember it. The purpose, of course, was to have many people work for me but to do it to open my heart. I fell into the lower vibration of *controlling*. I am not very proud of that lifetime. And I intend to repeat it.

Q: *Did you finish your contract?*

A: I finished some of it in that I had many people working for me. I just did not do it with *compassion* and *love*. I did it with *control*.

Q: *Will you go back with the same genetic entity and reincarnate? Do you understand what I mean?*

A: Do you mean with the same body? Or one that looks like it? *Yes.* NO, I do not want that body again! It has the multiple sclerosis genetic properties. I don't want that. I want a body that is stronger and not diseased.

Q: *Will you have a new vocation?*

A: In a way, yes. I will not be in *Communications* anymore, but I will still have to bring a great deal of people to me in the work place and hopefully deal with them in a kinder, more loving way.

Q: *Will you come back through a natural birth or will you come back as a walk-in?*

A: I am not quite sure what you mean as a *walk-in*. But I will be born into another set of parents. Is that what you mean?

Q: *That is the natural way but some souls have a contract with someone who is leaving his or her body and you would just take over.*

A: No, I would not want to do that—take on someone else's stuff. No thank you. I will just do it the natural way.

Q: *What was your biggest regret?*

A: I regret in not being kinder to people. That was part of my contract. I fell into the control, not really loving people. That is my regret—not having a bigger, deeper heart and being kinder to people.

Q: *So what are you being retrained about now?*

A: I had many belief systems about Hell and Bible teachings that were all wrong. I know now that I create my own Hell and that there is no such thing. I know now there is no such thing as sin, that I am my own creator.

Q: *My next question is whether you had met with past relatives, and you have already answered that.*

A: Yes, many relatives but not all that affected by them.

Q: *Have you met any other Masters besides Jesus?*

A: I know there were many Masters walking throughout, but I did not know their names. I could just see their energies and feel them as they went about their business, but I did not meet any more.

Q: *Have you seen any more pearly gates and streets paved with gold?*

A: No (*chuckles*); I know now that that is all a fable.

Q: *On Earth, did you believe in Hell?*

A: I believed what I was told, but certainly if you killed someone, you would go to Hell. I realize now that one's contract is so involved that maybe that was what the person was supposed to do, although I still have a hard time with that explanation.

Q: *So what dimension are you in now, since you are in the spirit form?*

A: I do not know.

Q: *Have you seen any new inventions, inventions that will be manifesting on Earth?*

A: I have seen some, but I am not allowed to talk about them. They are mainly in what I say the *travel department*, but we are cautioned not to describe them for we may describe them inaccurately. That gets carried down from Heaven and someone will create something that is not correct. So we were told to just not say anything.

Q: *I cannot think of any more questions particularly at this time.*

I thank you for coming, for giving me the honor of listening to your story and interviewing you. I am sure it will give the readers much information that they can ponder. Just as you have Angels in Heaven, I have Angels with Sananda who will escort you out of my space. I ask you not to return uninvited. I think you understand that I cannot have all these entities getting into my space to talk with me, for I am not that type of medium.

We were instructed about that, and I will honor that.

Thank you so much again for coming, using your code name of Rich-man. I wish you all the best for your next journey and send you much love and Light.

Thank you, my dear author of this book. You have a glorious aura.

Thank you (chuckling). I end this interview.

8:50 AM on 02-27-15.

*The etheric form that Rich-man had arrived in was no longer needed by him for identification. He had evolved enough so he could just be spirit now.

2 POOR-MAN

*G*ood *morning once again, my precious one. I am Sananda. So we come to chapter 2. You are excited and the Being we are calling* Poor-man *is excited and I am actually excited too.* Thank you for coming Sananda. *This will be a great chapter, so take some breaths, dear one; He is waiting and we will see what he has to say. 03-01-15, 7:20 AM.* Thank you, Sananda.

Hello ma'am. *Hello, greetings, thank you so much for coming. I have given you the code name of* Poor-man, *but that does not necessarily mean that you were. I am just using the nursery rhyme jingles for code names and to protect your anonymity.* I have already been clued into that. Where do you wish me to begin? *Why don't you start at your actual death process, what you remember of it?*

Actually, I try not to think too much about it. It was quite ugly in the end. During that time I got myself into a fix and did not know how to get out of it. You see, I took my own life—a suicide. I tied a rope around my neck, kicked the stool out from under me and by that time it was too late to say, *oh, I don't want to do this,* as I took my last gasp.

Life as I saw it had become unbearable for me. I was without funds for I had spent them on drugs and alcohol. I was an addict which I sorely regret. As I rest in Heaven, I see the error of my ways and what a waste I made of my life. I was only 32 when I took my life. While I had had women, I was not married. Thank God for that poor widow if I had had one. As I said, my death was quite ugly. I do not know how long I hung there before someone finally found me. I think it was probably my landlord, who was not of the highest consciousness either. You see, the rent was due and I did not have it. That was another one of my problems that added up to taking my life.

So I jumped off the stool to avoid him, but he did not find me until I had been dead many hours. Of course there was the furor about it all with the police, what have you. In the area I lived in where the addicts were, my suicide was not all that unusual. The police just murmured, *we've got another one; we've got a hanger.*

Then after the moments had passed and my body was dead, I remember the release. The body had gone through quite a struggle and when I—the spirit or whatever— was finally released from the body, it was such a relief! I remember standing and staring at what was my body. This *thing* that was emaciated and not what I would call a handsome man—all mottled with the death congealed blood…I just looked at it.

I then became aware that there were two Beings that were standing by me. I don't know how they got there. They just stood there. At times I felt I was talking to myself, for they didn't say anything. And then I said, *OK, that's it; I'm getting out of here.* With that I felt this whoosh and heard this whoosh in my ears, although I had no ears that I knew of. And I shot up. I went right through the ceiling, through the other apartments above me and out again. I went so fast that I could hardly get my bearings. I just zoomed upwards.

I didn't know where I was going, but I had heard all my life about Heaven and Hell. I had no doubt in my mind that I was going to Hell, and I was afraid. I was experiencing fear. I cursed and said, *damn, what have I done to myself. Damn, what a waste,* as I hurtled on up. The next thing I knew, I was no longer whooshing. I had come to some place. I was not sure whether I was in Hell or Heaven, and I was just waiting to find out.

The two men who were with me down on Earth, we'll say, were also there, which surprised me. And they were always waiting for me to speak first. They did not put words into my mouth. They just stood there. Then I said, *where in the hell am I?* They said, *where do you wish to be?* I said, *well, I sure as hell don't want to go there.* Then they said, *well then you won't, for you see, Hell is in your mind. That is your belief system. And since you have just said that you did not want to go there, you won't.* Then I said, *well, where in the hell will I go?* They said, *well, you better stop saying hell or you will go there.*

They said *had you ever thought of going to* Heaven? I replied that I did not think I was worthy enough to get into Heaven. I always thought of myself as a *loser.* You see, I have such little self-esteem—although I did not use that word; it was just in my head—I am not worthy; why would I go to Heaven? They very gently said to me, *my dear sir, you are worthy in the eyes of God; don't you know that?* They gave me so much love that I burst into tears (*Author: I am feeling goose bumps and tearful*). I said, *do I have to appear in front of God and the Judgment? I always have heard that would happen and now I am scared.* They said, *young sir...* They are always calling me *sir*; why do they do that? *Young sir, your body needs to be healed. Let's go to the Caring Center.* I replied, *what's that?* I am very suspicious because no one did anything for nothing from where I come from. *It is part of Heaven,* they replied. *You could say it is like a hospital-in-the-sky, although we do not term it as such. It is where you are cared for and healed.* I said *I do not have any money to pay for that.* They said, *you do not need money while in Heaven.*

They started using these endearing terms with me. They called me *dear sir* and *dear one*. I wasn't used to that and it made me feel funny. They just started walking toward the *Caring Center,* and I followed them for I did not know where else to go; I was afraid of getting lost. I thought that I had so many fears: I was afraid of being alone; I was afraid of getting lost; I was afraid that nobody loved me. I was just afraid all the time. Then I said to myself, *damn you, you weren't afraid to kill yourself.*

The men—I will call them men, but I can't say for sure—read my thoughts and said, *dear one, each time you damn yourself, you are harming yourself. Come, you will find in the* Caring Center *all of your cares and worries in that past life will be faded away.*

I could barely believe that! How was that so? So I followed them and went into this place. It was overwhelming, for it was so peaceful and filled with love. All of this I had not experienced before. It was too much. I could not go any further. I said, *wait; this is not the right place. I can't take this. I can't go any further.* They took my arms and kept talking to me and walking me along. Since they had my arms, I kept walking also. Pretty soon we came to this nice room. The sun was shining; the birds were chirping—all of this I did not have back home. So I stood for a while by the window and again I started feeling so grateful, but put it in my way of speaking, swearing again, *God damn, I wonder how much this room costs!*

They led me to what looked like a bed and they said, *you have had a long journey—a painful and tiring journey.* They said, *lie down now and sleep and rest and sleep again.* I said, *can I have something to drink? I don't suppose you have any hard stuff—certainly not any champagne because that would be celebrating something. I am not celebrating; I just want something to drink to calm my nerves.* And they brought me a glass of very clear, cold water and said, *drink some of this. You are thirsty; you need some cool liquid. It is not alcohol, but it will taste very good.* I took a couple of gulps because I was thirsty. My mouth felt dry. It tasted so good, I just drank the whole thing and gave the glass back—I'll call it a glass, but it was a glass like I had never seen before. It looked like it was in the shape of a tulip. I gave it back to them and again they urged me to lie down and rest.

So I flopped down on the bed and noted how comfortable it was. I had not had a bed like that since I can remember, if I ever even had one. I kicked off my dirty, worn shoes, thinking, *how come I still have shoes on when I am dead.* Then the next thing I knew, I rested.

Later I was told I had lain there and was healed, as much as could be healed in that session, with music…They used crystals which I thought were pretty, but I did not know much about them. The bed was cozy and warm; it had been a long time since I had had a bed I could wrap myself in. It felt wonderful. When I awoke, I was so refreshed. I didn't look around for a beer bottle as I did at home, although I don't want to call that home anymore. I don't want ever to go back there.

You see, in my head I still get kind of mixed up. I don't know whether I am alive or dead. I remember jumping off the stool and strangling myself, so I have to be dead and yet I am alive. Look! I still have a body and still have on the same clothes; I am alive. So all of these things are going through my head. Then I laid down and went to sleep.

When I awoke, I was still in what is known as the *Caring Center.* I had a robe on and did not know how that happened. I thought, *well somebody must have taken my clothes off. I hope it wasn't a girl.* I was aware that I was ashamed. I had not bathed and I was smelly. I just did not want a girl to smell me and see me. My beard was all straggly. I didn't have a tooth brush so I hadn't brushed my teeth. And yet I had to say to myself, *that is all past.* The man next to me, who I found out is an Angel, said to me, *yes that is past, dear one. Those thoughts are not real for you anymore. Those are your Earth thoughts; they are not real. This is real. You are in a section of Heaven. You are in the* Care Center *and you are on the same floor with many others who were in similar straits that you were in.* They took me into a room and here were all these other, I'll call, *derelicts.* You could tell that they had had a rough time in their lifetimes. Then we just all started talking and telling our stories, telling each other how we had taken our lives; how we wanted a drink, or how we <u>had</u> wanted one; how we wanted another shot. So we told our stories and we found that we were not alone.

Each one of us was dressed in a different colored robe. We found out later that the colors in those robes were giving off different energies that would heal us. Those in fear wore blue robes, for that color was very peaceful. Those who had the vilest types of death by someone else wore green because they were still healing. And on it went.

There is no-time there, so I do not know how long I spent there. The Angel that came with me from Earth was still there. He told me he was what is known as my *Master Guide.* He had always been with me from the time of my birth.

Many of the words I use now are new to my vocabulary. I was not all that educated while on Earth and did not know how to speak well. I understand I am speaking to the Author of this book I am telling my story to. I can tell from her energy that she is very educated and I was not. I am in awe that she would even allow me near her for she is so far above me. The Angels are stepping in and telling me that I am putting myself down. There is no lesser God. *You are all Gods in your own right. Your aura is being healed. Your memory banks are being*—they use the term *recalibrated,* but I do not know what that meant—my thoughts were changing. I noticed that I did not swear any more. I made no (this is a new term for me) concentrated *effort* to change. I just did. I think it must have been that Caring Center, for when

I woke up, I spoke differently and was thinking differently. Things seemed to just change.

When I was in this group with people who had similar lifetimes, I could see the changes in them and therefore, I knew there were similar changes in me. My Master Guide said, *you see you are being what we call retrained; you are being healed.*

I can't think of much more to say to you. I understand you will ask me questions. That's fine with me for you know much more than I do. Oh, I know what else I want to say. I no longer think of where I used to live on Earth as home. That is no longer home to me; this is Home; this is Home now. I don't know what I will do again. I don't know what is expected of me here—what they will do with me, so I just go on from day to day. I was in our group and we knew there was a chance you could go back again. They called it *reincarnation*. I had some fear about that. I did not want to go back to that body. I did not want to go back as a dog or cat. I even heard you could go back as a mouse or something. I did not want to do that.

I did not know what to expect. I did not know enough. So I asked to be…They call it being *retrained* on that so I would have more information and they told me about *reincarnation,* and that it was my choice as to what I wanted to do, if I wanted to repeat that lifetime…

They said I could even go back as a woman if I wished. I thought, why would I want to do that? Then I really would have problems—a man being a woman. I don't think I would like that. I just did not know enough about all of this stuff.

So I don't know what else to say so I'll just say fire away on your questions. That will raise up more ideas.

Questions (Q) & Answers (A)

All right, these are some of the simple questions I have asked other(s).

Q: You have told us you were 32 when you died, so how long has it been since you last had a body—how long have you been in Heaven?

A: I don't know 'cause it's not in Time, but I don't think it has been very long 'cause there is still so much I do not know.

Q: What form do you have now; what are you in now?

A: I don't know what you mean by form. Do you mean do I have a body? *Yes.* Yes, I have a body just like I had before, although I would like to have another one, for I was not very handsome and I would like to be a handsome man; so I still have that body.

Q: When souls take bodies, they have a purpose. What was your purpose in that lifetime?

A: I don't know; I don't know what my purpose was.

Q: Did you finish your contract?

A: No; we did have an overview of our life, or review you call it. It was too painful to look at and I don't want to talk about it. They told us we had a contract, but I don't want to talk about it; I don't know what mine was.

Q: If you decide to reincarnate will you just take that same body?

A: Actually I want a different body; I want to be a man and I want to be more handsome than I was. I was kind of tall and skinny. I just would like to be more muscular—more masculine, I guess you would say.

Q: Will you be born again via the natural process through a woman or will you jump into someone else's body and take their contract?

A: I don't know what you mean by all of that. Of course I'll just get born again.

Q: What was your biggest regret in that lifetime?

A: I think my biggest regret was I took my life too soon. If I was going to commit suicide, why didn't I wait for 10 years? Maybe by then I wouldn't have to do it. Maybe I would have hooked up with a woman and she would not have let me kill myself. Or maybe I would have joined a religion, or something like that. But my biggest regret is I killed myself too soon. (*He sounded sad.*)

Q: So what are you being retrained about now?

A: You mean like schooling where they are taking me to different areas to learn different things?

Yes, that's a possibility.

They talk about what I think, what I believe. Then they give me other ideas so is that what you mean by retraining? *Yes, that's part of it.* So in that sense we have talked about the difference between Heaven and Hell and that Hell was all of my own doing and beliefs and my own actions. I found out I actually was already in Hell just in that lifetime. You can't be an alcoholic and/or a drug addict and not say it was a Hell. It was a hell of a life. I hated it.

Q: Have you met with any of your past relatives, those who have died before you?

A: I have met some of them, but I did not really know them, so I can't say it was any great joy to me or not. It was just *oh, so you're* (anonymity*). OK, and your name was what? Oh, you were my Aunt...? Oh, I didn't know I had an Aunt... And you are who?* It sort of just went on like that. I can't say it was very, uh, enlightening, shall we say.

Q: Have you met any of whom are called the *Ascended Masters*?

A: Well there was Jesus. I saw him from a distance. You can't help but see him when he comes with such a Light that everybody starts running to this Being and saying, *he's come; he's come!* I look up and see this tremendous Light. It is like going toward a search light or a light in the ball park or something like that. Then everybody is saying, *it's him; it's him.* And I am saying who is *"him?"* And they are saying *that's Jesus!* So I did not meet him but saw him from a distance.

Q: Did you attend your own funeral or memorial?

A: I'm not sure; I had no funeral. They just took me to the morgue, so I guess I would have to say, no. But I was present when they took my body away. I don't know how I got there. I just was. Maybe I saw it on the screens; I don't know. I don't like to look at those pasts. They make me sad, then I am angry. They make me think too much. I just don't like it.

Q: So you can just view things on a screen?

A: Oh, yes, there is a room you can go to and view anything that you wish, say Egypt. There would be all of the pyramids and you would see all of that. You could go back to the beginning and see the history of it and follow it through. You could see anything. So I would go see on the screen all the different countries I had wanted to travel to. I liked places like Egypt that you have heard about. I liked Africa. I did not like seeing all the slaves. They were black but they were in similar situations as I was and I did not like watching them. But I liked watching the animals as they roamed so freely. I loved all of that.

Q: How did you come to me; what was that procedure?

A: A very high Being sought me out; I do not know why. He was high because I could tell by his Light. He came to me and asked me if I would tell my story to someone who was writing a book. I said, *of course, why not*. By this time just being in my group of other addicts, it meant nothing to me to go tell it to someone else.

Q: So when you came to me, how did you get here?

A: My Angel Guide brings me; I don't know how. It's like one minute I am in Heaven and the next minute I am here.

Q: How far into my energy field do you come?

A: They told me I would know when I could go no further because there was an energy gate where I could go no further; it just kind of stopped. That's where I am; I don't know where it is. So they told me then to just listen to you and tell my story and answer your questions.

Thank you so much.

Q: Am I correct in saying you have not channeled to others before?

A: No, I have not; you are the first one.

I am honored.

You are honored to be talking to an addict who has killed himself?

Yes, I am; it is a great honor and I thank you.

Well, that's a first!

Q: How long have you been in Heaven?

A: I haven't a clue.

Q: Do you have a job with a title to it?

A: Do you mean like the garbage man or the dishwasher or something like that?

Q: Well I don't think those would be the jobs, but they do have different things that people do.

A: No, I pretty much just wander around. I came out of the Care Center and my Guides took me to the room where I meet with this group.

Q: So do you hang out with that group much of the time now?

A: Yes, they are friends now. We all know each other's stories and there is comfort in that. Sort of like we are alike so we don't have fears; we don't feel unworthy or less than. In other words, someone like yourself would not be associating with our group. You are much higher—evolved I guess you would say. You would not be in our group. You could be there as a teacher maybe, but you would not be a part of that group.

Q: Do you watch events on Earth on a screen or something?

A: Oh yes; there is a place where you can go and watch what is going on. I like to watch the ball games and fight-nights. You can watch anything on the screen of what is going on on Earth. And I am just so glad to be here. I don't ever want to go back.

Q: Describe your living quarters. Do you live in an apartment or in a dormitory? How is that set up? Do you live with your group?

A: We stay pretty close together. We have what you would call a *dormitory.* We chose that because we wanted to be together. Each of us has his own group. There were no women in our group so there are just males. Each of us has his own room; it is very comfortable—certainly better than the apartment I had on Earth. It is very simple; what you would call *monk-like.* There is a comfortable chair and a bed.

Are there wash stands, or bathing facilities?

We do not have any of those body functions but there is a large area. I guess you could call it a bathing area. It is like a large swimming pool and you can jump into that. There is soap there if you want to soap yourself down. Some do it simply because they did not have it while on Earth. But it is not to cleanse particularly but to just feel the water; it is so clean.

So you live in this dormitory and there is a large swimming area, we'll call it. Yes. *And is there a food court and/or a kitchen? Do you still eat?*

Oh yes, we eat all the things we were not able to eat while on Earth. Most of us did not have the money to do so because we used it all on alcohol or drugs. Of course none of that is allowed here in Heaven, so we have a dining hall. It is open all the time. You can go in any time and have your water. They also have a very delicious tea, I found out.

I never thought I would be a tea-drinker but this is quite good. And there is anything that you wish to eat. Of course there is no meat, but we are learning to eat salads and vegetables. I like the mashed potatoes. They give me comfort. I guess you call that *comfort food*. I like macaroni and cheese, different vegetables, soups and breads. I am learning to be a baker, actually. I like punching the dough and making the breads. I could do that if I went back to Earth. I had not thought of that. I could be a Baker!

Q: Do you still need water and food or do you just drink it and eat it because you like it?

A: I never thought about that. When it's time to eat we just go eat, or we feel like it's time to eat. I know there are others here in Heaven who do not eat, but we haven't figured out how they get away with that. They look strong and healthy and they don't eat anything. I don't get it. But I am with my group and I am happy and I am feeling joy in being here. I hope I am here for a long time. I know there will be a time when my Angels will guide me and talk more about reincarnation and what you want to do next and what is expected of you. But it is just too overwhelming right now. I don't even want to think about it.

All right; is there anything you wish to say to me right now, because we are coming to the end of this interview?

I can't think of anything but I really have had a good time and I thank you for bringing me to you. I don't know how that is done, but I thank you.

You are welcome and it has been my honor, Poor-man, *and that is just a code name.*

I think in many ways I was a poor man, but I don't think that anymore.

That is good, for that code-name is just a nursery rhyme. You are blessed, you know. So I thank you for coming. This interview is now finished. I wish you all the best! And when you return to Earth, have a great life and remember you are loved. You are not the lesser God. You are loved. I give you my greatest gratitude and love. I wish you a great journey.

Thank you so much, great Being. I don't know who you are but someday I shall. Thank you, goodbye.

Goodbye.

8:20 AM. Well Sananda, he really lived up to that name, didn't he?

But that is a judgment, isn't it? *Oh you poor man.* It was not meant to be like that, but it did seem to fit.

Thank you for bringing him, Sananda. It certainly was different.

Yes, and that is what this book is all about, dear one—the versatility and all the different journeys that the souls have gone through. Alright, dear one, until we bring in chapter 3 and that will be the *Beggar-man.*

Oh-oh that will even top this one, perhaps (chuckles). *Thank you, Sananda.*

You are welcome, dear one. Over and out.

3 BEGGAR-MAN

H ello, *and hello to you.* I will be the third man in your Chapter 3, and I believe you have given me the code name of *Beggar-man.* *Yes, that is correct.* I had a quite interesting death. I had been ill. I was a young man in my twenties, and I had been ill and none of the healers knew what was wrong with me. So they brought me the usual priests and healers to come over and pray. They even brought shamans to do their magic. Nothing worked. So I decided that if I was going to get better, I needed to change my ways.

I was a gambler and in your time period, it was around the 1800's, I used to go to this gambling house. Some would call it a *whore-house.* I hope that does not shock you, readers, but I gambled and I whored.

During that time, I met a woman who was quite delightful. I can say honestly that she was, up to that point, the only one who seemed to truly love me for who I was. She knew my body was ill. None of us knew why. So she started taking care of me. She saw to it that I ate well; she saw to it that I lessened my drinking. She saw to it that I had more sleep and she, we could say, quit her job and only took care of my needs.

During that time my body healed, and it showed me that there was something in this teaching of clean life and clean living. In my gambling I had saved enough money—this too was in her cautioning, *you've got to save some money, honey. You don't want to do this all your life.*

In those days you bought a little farm, raised some cattle, or if you were a sheep man, raised some sheep, or just raised some chickens. I was able to save enough and we bought a small farm in what you would call the *mid-west*. The winters were fierce but the other seasons were quite pleasant. It wasn't a large farm but one that produced; we could sell our vegetables; we had some fruit trees too; we sold our meat and we got along very nicely. We had two sons and life was good.

I lived quite a few more years and then one day, I had an accident. I know you say there is no such thing as an accident, but we did not know that then. I was out with the stock. My horse bolted; I was thrown. A calf we were trying to rope skittered and by accident kicked out and kicked me in the head. I was, oh, I guess—you see we lost track of time so we really did not know our birthdays—I think maybe I was in my early 40's. My wife was about 10 years younger.

So here I am lying in the dirt with a kicked-in brain, bleeding from the nose because it was broken too. I remember thinking, *is this it? Is this how I am going to die?* Then I heard a voice say, *you're already dead, dear soul.* I know now that was my Guardian Angel. But, you see, I was still kind of stuck in the body. I could not get out and my Guardian Angel said, *just let go and kind of slip out.* So as he or she or whoever said that, I remembered kind of feeling like I had relaxed the hold on myself.

The next thing I knew, I was standing next to this man who I now know was my Angel and he said *OK, you did it.* I said, *did what?* He replied, *you died! You have been trying for twenty years and you finally made it.* I was kind of confused by that because I remembered seeing my smashed-up body and smelling the steers and feeling the dirt and noting the blue sky, the chickens pecking away. So I said, *OK, what do we do now?* The Angel said, *what do you think you are going to do now?* I said, *well, I've got to go tell my wife* (I know we aren't supposed to say any names.). He said, *yes, you could do that.*

The next thing I know…I don't know how I got there…I was standing beside her and I was saying…let's give her a name…let's call her *Lucy.* So I said, *Lucy, I'm gone, baby!* And there was no answer. She was darning some socks, and she never even looked up. I said to the Angel who was also there, *she didn't say anything. She can't hear me! She didn't respond!* And the Angel said, *that's because you are dead, my young man, and she is not hearing you from that dimension.*

I tried touching her and poking her, and I noticed my hand just kind of went through her arm. Well, I was getting very agitated because I wanted to hold her and say goodbye and to say I was sorry. I was getting very engulfed in my emotions. I was almost screaming at her. *Lucy! Honey! Can't you hear me?* Then I started sobbing and said, *goodbye, my love; thank you for my life.* Then I said to the Angel, *OK, just get me the hell out of here.*

The next thing I knew, I was kind of traveling like on a speed train, although there was no train. There was this tunnel I had always heard about. I was in this tunnel, and it was kind of dark but it wasn't black. I can't explain it. It was dark, but you could see through it. It was not like a night-time dark. All the time I am speeding along—sort of like traveling (*by train*) through a mountain—and noticed there was a light at the end.

The next thing I knew, I had stopped and I was in a brilliant light. My guides said, *OK, we're here.* I looked around and kind of mumbled, *where is "here"?* He said, *don't you know?* I said, *I am not sure; I do not see pearly* gates *and hear all this music, so I guess it is not Heaven; but I do not see fires and hear cries of anguish so I don't know where I am.* The Angel said, *have you ever heard of the* Netherlands—*the* Shadow-lands? I thought he was talking about the physical Earth. *Yeah, I've been there lots of times, but you don't want to raise cattle there. They need some sun.* My guide said, *no, I am not speaking of Earth. I am speaking where you as a soul hover between two worlds. Your soul does not know which way to go—whether to go to Heaven or whether to go to Hell. You carry so many belief systems.*

You are so mixed up in your head that there is no clear passage. You believe you ought to be in Hell for the excessive drinking, the whoring, the fights and the unthinkable things you thought you had done. And yet there is a part of you that wants to see pearly gates and streets of gold.

Whenever there were clergy men who came to the villages and held these tent singings and sermons, you always went. You were interested to hear what they had to say, but they spent so much time on damnation *that you left and felt like a total victim to all of that. So where do you want to go? This is a choice for you. It is almost like a rest stop. Where do you want to go?*

Well, I don't want to go to Hell—Heaven sakes, no! I want to go to Heaven. I believe in God; I just want to see some of the glorious things I have heard about all my life.

The next thing, there I was. I exclaimed, *oh, it is magnificent; look at the gates! They are all pearls!* And I peaked through the gates for they weren't open yet and I said, *Oh my gosh, look at the streets; they are all gold. This really is true.* There was a magnificent Being by the gate with robes on and a long beard. I said, *you must be St. Peter* and he said in a very deep voice, *if you wish me to be.*

Well I didn't understand that so I said, *why are the gates shut? Can't I go in?* He replied, *do you believe you can go in?* I said, *well if someone opens them for me I can.* He said again, *are you asking me to open these gates for you?* I said, *oh yes; I want to see all of these glories that I have been told about.* Therefore, the gates opened. I only took a couple of steps in when I was so overpowered by the magnificence of it and the beauty of it that I was just struck still. I was just in awe. I just stared.

I found I could not move forward and I turned to find my Angel and saw that he was standing outside the gates. So I practically ran back to him and said, *it is magnificent; why didn't you come with me?* He just looked at me and smiled. He said, *do you believe all of that you are seeing?* I remember just kind of pausing. *Well, the preacher-man who came to the village talked about it. He took it right out of the Bible, so I believed that. But now that I see it, I guess I believe it, but it is too much for me. I can't handle it. I have never lived in riches like that. I don't want to live in a place like that. It is too much for me. I just want an open range and some cattle like it used to be. I can't live like that.*

Then the guide said, *turn around.* I did and it wasn't there anymore. I exclaimed, *hey, what's going on here? Am I sick; are those headaches back again? What's happened?* The guide explained, *all that you saw was an illusion. It was in your belief system and in your mind. It was not real.* I exclaimed, *this is too weird; this is just too weird!* I remember just kind of sitting, slumping down with my head between my hands. Then I noticed that my head was not all that bashed in after all; my nose was kind of crooked, but it wasn't bleeding. *Oh, something is going on here.*

With that my guide said, *come; I am taking you to the Caring Center so that you can be healed more and rest. All will become clear to you in a little while.* By this time I felt tired and I was so confused. I missed Lucy and my kids—the dog and the farm. So I just followed him; I just needed to lie down and get healed.

I followed along, and he took me to the Caring Center which was in a magnificent building. I said to myself, *don't look; this is an illusion also.* The Angel who was with me could read my mind, and he said, *no this is not an illusion. You are in Heaven and this is real. This is a Caring Center. You will be healed here. Come.*

And I followed him, just like a lamb follows her mother-sheep. He said, *come, lie down.* He took me into this room that had soothing music and what looked like sunlight coming through a window and a comfortable bed. I felt like I was all muddy and dirty. He said, *just take off your clothes and boots and crawl into bed. Don't worry about anything anymore.* So I tore off my clothes that were still kind of bloody and my dirty old boots and just crawled in between the sheets. I noticed they were flannel sheets like I have at home. Everything was so comfortable, and I laid down on a pillow and thought of home and Lucy. But I was so tired; I just went to sleep.

The next thing I remember is that I awoke and I was in a green robe. I felt very refreshed. I felt my face and it felt like it used to be. I was hungry and just felt good. I got out of bed and noticed there were like sandals to put on my feet. I looked around and there was my Angel guide.

I said, as I stretched, *oh, that felt better. How long was I sleeping?* The guide said there is no time here but on Earth's time you were probably here two weeks. *Two weeks! Oh, my gosh.* I then thought of home again and I thought, *oh, my poor wife. She has to take care of that farm all by herself.* I then heard a voice in my head that said, *she will be fine; she will be fine.*

As I thought about it, I remembered… I think I had a dream where I went to her. It was my funeral. There were my neighbors. There was a preacher-man and they said nice things about me. They brought food, but my Lucy was crying most the time. My sons were very subdued. It is all I remember about that dream. My angels said, *yes, we took you there. It was a short visit, but you saw people mourning you and saying nice things about you. You needed to hear that you were a good man. Now you have more healing to do.*

I said, *what else?* He said, *now we are going to another building.* He took me to this other building and led me into this room where there was a huge screen. He told me I was going to view the life I had had. I said, *oh, my gosh, why would I want to do that?* Then I said, *oh, I have heard of this. The preacher-man would talk about this.*

And sure enough it had already started—as soon as I had approached the screen, it had started. There I was as a baby, and it came on through to my death. I saw everything about me. I saw everything I had done to other people and everything that others had done to me. The worst times seemed to be when I was a teenager and I got into a bad crowd.

We had learned to shoot and we went around shooting birds and firing in the sky. I never killed anybody, so I did not have to see that. But I was so glad when I came out of there. It is draining to sit there and see and feel at the same time everything you are seeing. I said, *OK, enough already; I don't want to talk about it anymore.*

The next thing I knew, the Angel took me to another building and to this room. There were quite a few people in there. They were all telling what had happened to them and how they had died. They seemed to be all around the same age. There were only men. We all greeted each other and there were sort of name-tags and we all wrote our names or made our X's, stuck them on us so that as we went from one person to the next, we could call them by name. There was one Being that seemed to be in charge. We could tell he was more educated than we were—I'll say higher than we were. He was like a teacher. He asked us questions, and we told how we had died and how the review had gone for us. We started meeting and we became friends.

I don't have much more to say. I'll just leave it up to you now.

All right, thank you. You do know that the code-name Beggar-man was just given to you in order to keep this anonymous so no one would recognize you.

Yes, I was instructed on that and that you would be asking me some questions.

Yes, this is the time of the Q & A, questions and answers.

Questions (Q) & Answers (A)

You have already said you were around the early forties when you died. *Yes.*

Q: So how long has it been since you have had a body?

A: *Well I guess that is where you get to do the math for I am not quite sure. They say it was around the 1800's.*

Q: So what form do you have now? Do you know what I mean by that?

A: *Do you mean am I a ghost or what?*

Q: Well, I guess that is some type of form, but do you have a body or are you in spirit energy?

A: *Oh I have a body. It is very similar to the one I had back home, but I am not supposed to say that anymore. This is Home.*

Q: When you had your review, did the Angels talk to you about what your purpose was in that lifetime?

A: *No, I don't quite know what you mean by that.*

Q: When we take a body, we have contracts. Did you have a contract?

A: *Oh, I see what you mean. Let's see—my contract was I was supposed to meet Lucy. And my contract was… Oh, I had not seen that before. I was supposed to die when I was 41. Well, I guess I did that!*

Q: In your review did you talk about reincarnation?

A: *Not in the review, but when we were meeting all together with that teacher, we talked about reincarnation.*

Q: And will you reincarnate? Do you wish to go back and have the same body that you had before?

A: *Oh no, I don't want that body. There was something wrong with it, for it got so sick. I know we have a choice whether to be a male or female but I don't think I would want it to be a female. I would not be used to that. I will go back and have a male body.*

Q: Will you have some type of vocation like a… What would you say you would like to be? Do you want to work in a printer shop, be a baker, a farmer, or lawyer or anything like that?

A: *Well, I know I will have to be very educated. Actually, I have always wanted to be a surgeon. Now that sounds kind of funny. I know when I was on the farm and worked with my animals, they would get, you know, cuts on wire and things like that. I would sew them up and think to myself that would be fun to be a doctor and be a surgeon. So yeah, I think I would like to be a surgeon.*

Q: What was your biggest regret?

A: *Oh, my biggest regret was in leaving Lucy.*

Q: Yes, I know that must be difficult. Do you have a regret about what you could have done more or less when you had that lifetime?

A: *Oh, I see what you mean. Well, I guess I could have had more education. I could not read very well, but Lucy could. I could sign my name and did not have to use an X. I never could quite figure out what good an X would do. Anyway I never did that. Yes that is what I would have to do—have more education. I could be nicer to people. Sometimes I was kind of surly and did not treat them very well. So I could have been nicer. I want to have some humor. I want to be able to make a mistake and laugh about it—not that it was so horrible, but (I will give myself a name and say* John*) gosh,* John, you're all fingers today. *Kind of make a joke about it. Instead I would say,* damn it John, pay attention. *I want to change that.*

Q: Have you met with any past relatives?

A: *Oh, there's been a few. You know it seems that so many people died in that era, as I look back at that. You couldn't keep up with them. So now that I am in Heaven, I see them once in a while. I see past relatives, but they do not mean that much to me. I did not have any particular girlfriends except Lucy. I'd like to have a life with her, a proper life, if I get the chance, where we meet as teenagers and she does not have to whore in order to have money and stay alive. She was a pretty woman. You can't say she was beautiful, but she had a beautiful heart. She loved me, and that was all that mattered.*

Q: We are coming to the end of our interview. Is there anything you would like to ask or say to me personally?

A: *No, not in particular, but I appreciate your having chosen me for an interview. I do not know why, but it made me feel kind of special, and I like that feeling. I have been told that you are writing a book and my experiences will be in the book. That's kind of fun for me to know. I understand, though, that there are no names other than the codes you have given them. So you don't know any of the people. And I won't know any of them either, but I hope to read your book someday. Maybe when I return to my life on Earth again, I will be able to read your book—not that I will remember, for I understand your memory is erased when you come back again. But I thank you; it has been a great time and I have enjoyed it.*

And I thank you for coming and speaking so freely of your past. I feel honored that you would come, and I wish you all the best for your next lifetime. May God bless all of your endeavors. So I bid you farewell and this interview is now at an end. Goodbye.

Goodbye!

Wow, Sananda, one from the Wild, Wild West, we could say.

Yes, I thought it would be interesting for the readers to know that not everyone reincarnates right away, since there is no time. And he is still there. All right, dear one, enjoy typing it up.

Thanks, Sananda; I am not sure when we'll meet again; this week is pretty busy, but I thank you.

You are welcome, dear one. Over and out, with love.

Thank you, Sananda, love to you, too. Good bye.

Good bye.

8:20 AM, 03-03-15.

4 THIEF-MAN

03-06-15 at 7:20 AM. Hello, precious one, bright and early I see, or right on time to bring in your next chapter. Yes, Lord. Now this Chapter 4 has the code name of Thief-man, although that does not necessarily mean that was his past life. I will step back now and let him step forward, for he is eagerly waiting to speak with you. Thank you, Sananda.

Oh, I am so excited; I have never done this before. Hello great Being! *Well, hello to you too, and thank you for the compliment* (chuckles). *You have been instructed on how this works?* Yes, I have and I am very eager to get started. *All right then, I will turn this over to you and you can start telling me and the readers your story.*

I want to go back to when I was a baby. My mother had a difficult birth and the family kind of hovered over me. I was what you might call a *spoiled child*. I had temper tantrums. I soon found that if I used my temper, I could get anything I wanted when I wanted. I grew up and was given a good education and went on to college. I excelled in sports, actually, but I soon found that while the sports were gratifying, they did not feed me intellectually. I wanted to learn more. I studied and studied and ended up with a major in history. (This is a little aside here, but since I am in Heaven, they almost have to tear me away from the screens because I am enjoying all the histories I can see happening. It is like a continuous movie. Anyway, I am getting ahead of myself.) I am spending days on end in the campus library reading up on history. Then I graduated and did not know what I was going to do (*as a vocation*). The only thing a history major could do was a librarian job, although now-a-days that is getting to be pretty scarce because nobody reads books that you can hold. They are all into Kindle and e-books. But anyway, that's kind of another aside. I did not know what I was going to have as a vocation to bring in some money.

I realized there was not all that stuff open for a history major. So since my family was quite wealthy, I decided to heck with trying to work my vocation, I would just start traveling. My family let me book these different cruises, but they were not the ordinary cruises where everyone is wining and dining. These were in less luxurious ships—freighters— for I wanted to get *down and dirty,* so to speak, when we came into port. I wanted to get closer to it all. I learned so much more about the country because so many of the people of the countries I visited were also part of the freighter crew. That's what I wanted, not the luxurious wining and dining of the cruise ships.

I kept hopping from one freighter to another—hopping from one glorious country to another. I found I was happiest in the tropical countries with the dense foliage. A lot of people could not stand the humidity, but it did not seem to bother me. I was one who seemed never to put on weight so that I did not feel that hot and uncomfortable all the time. Yes, I perspired, but you just get used to that and take along extra antiperspirant, etc.

Life was interesting, and I did all the things that visitors and *delvers* into the different cultures did. Yes, I tried the drugs. They were OK while they lasted, but I didn't like the aftermath, so I soon quit that. I drank alcohol in moderation because I did not like the after-effects of that either—to be hung over with a headache all day long. So I was able to modify the drugs that I used. I did not want to become an addict.

Life was zooming along pretty well, and then I hit what you call a *bump in the road*. I was touring the jungle and all of that when the driver lost control of the Landrover, and we rolled and rolled. (*The truck*) did not have a very sturdy roof—nothing but canvas. I realized as I laid there that I had broken my neck. The driver also was injured fairly severely, but there were natives in the area who soon found us and reported it (*our accident*) to the authorities.

We were carted away to a make-shift hospital. I was fortunate there was a doctor who spoke halting English, for by this time I could not move and he told me that I would be paralyzed for the rest of my life. Of course, that just flabbergasted me. That was probably the worst message anyone could receive.

They contacted my parents, and my father flew down, assessed the situation, and had me air-evacuated. When the American doctors examined me, they had even less enthusiasm, for there was no hope.

I remember lying in my bed and thinking, *wouldn't be wonderful to just close my eyes, go to sleep, and wake up in Heaven?* I had no doubt I would go to Heaven. My life was fairly clean. I had some women but more of a necessity than anything—sort of a *one-nighter*, so to speak, some *afternooners*. Anyway, I went to sleep.

When I awoke, I was in the same hospital bed, but I did not seem to be in the hospital. I didn't get it. I heard music, and there were other sounds. There were these huge crystals laying all over the floor. There was this soft light beaming on me, and I remember thinking to myself, *I don't remember that they had crystals in the room.* I guess I must have been out of it—you know in that hospital room. I kind of dozed and went back to sleep.

The next time I awoke, there was a man there who I assumed was the male nurse; he had a robe on, which I thought was kind of funny. He said, *all right, let's go into another room.* I said, *but I am paralyzed; I can't move.* He said, *yes, you can; sit up.* I was following his orders, so I sat up; then I plopped down again; then I sat up again and said, *oh, my God, I can sit up! I'm not paralyzed from the waist up.* He sort of smiled and said, *all right, now stand up.*

I said, *you mean I can stand up too? I am not paralyzed?* And he said *no, you were healed while you slept.* I said *boy, that was some healing I had then. How long did I sleep?* He smiled and said, *oh, quite a few days, sir. Days?!* He said, *actually it was weeks. Weeks?!* And he said, *don't you know where you are?* I looked around and there was my hospital bed and windows with some light going through it. I said, *I don't remember. I just know they had a lot of tubes in me, and I don't remember any crystals. Look, I am wearing this green robe; where are my clothes?* He said, *your clothes were taken off of you because they still had the effects of your accident.*

Oh, that's right, I was in that car accident. We rolled. God, that was awful! I then turned to the man and said, *so what's your name? Who are you?* He said, *I am your* Guardian Angel. I started laughing, *yeah, right; well you certainly are my* Guardian Angel *if you got me out of bed. Ok, so where are we going? First of all, where am I now; is this another part of the hospital?* He replied, *well, you could call it the* hospital-in-the-sky *if you wish. Actually, it is a Caring Center.* I said, *oh, ok, they moved me into a place for paraplegics then.* The man said *no, this is a* Caring Center and then said, *follow me,* and I followed him into another section. (The Angel observed that he still did not know he was dead. He felt so well, you see; he just felt so well.)

So the man led me into this room where all the screens are and immediately the screen was playing my past life. I still didn't get it.

I exclaimed at all the scenes. *Oh, wow, this is wonderful; somebody has a TV record with my whole life on it. These are wonderful pictures; wait until I tell Mom and Dad.*

I started to see and feel my life and its total completeness. I saw the *accident* where the truck driver had lost control and the truck rolled several times. I felt that. I was moaning and saying, *oh no; oh no, I'm going to be killed! Oh no*! Then the screen showed how my father came and air-evacuated me back to the States and to the hospital there. (It still had not dawned on me that I had died.) I said, *I remember going to sleep and just saying wouldn't be nice to just go to sleep and wake up in Heaven.* But I said, *here I am looking at a movie about my life. This is kind of neat, although it was very hurtful in spots, but it's neat. OK, man, what's next?*

He said, *all right, follow me.* We went into another building, and it was a room with other people (who did not know they had died either).

The facilitator came in and started greeting people. They all put their name-tags on and started telling their stories. They talked about where they had a horrible experience that would have killed a regular person but *whew, I am still here!* Then another person told his story. Someone said, *whoa, what's wrong with this picture? Do you think those accidents we had were not really accidents but our death processes?* Others just kind of jerked around and stared. *What do you mean? I mean do you think that we all died?* Someone yelled, *oh for Christ' sake! I don't believe in all that crap.* The facilitator asked, *you don't believe in what? I don't believe we could all be talking like this and be dead!*

The facilitator asked, *what do you believe? I don't know, but I don't feel dead, so I did not die.* The facilitator asked, *anyone else have any comments?* Someone said, *well, if we died, why can't we actually remember we died? Why can't we remember going through a tunnel or something like that?* The facilitator said, *do any of you remember going through a tunnel?* Everybody shook their head, no. No, it was like I blanked out; I was unconscious and when I woke up there was this medical aide—medical nurse—and he just sort of led me around, led me to this group. The facilitator said, *that man is your Guardian Angel. Yeah, right,* somebody said. *I have always heard we have Guardian Angels, but he does not have any wings on; he looks just like us. By the way, we all have on these weird robes. What's that about? How did we get these?*

The facilitator sort of explained, *well, when you came here and you were unconscious, we took your clothes off and put you in a robe and put you to sleep, to heal.* He said, *oh, Ok.*

Then we started just chattering away and asking what each did (*vocation*) and did they have a family, kids, and all of that. It got on the subject of *hey, did you go to the room where your whole life was on a screen?* And they all started speaking at once. *Yes!* The facilitator asked, *have your heard about people who have passed having their life review?* There was silence—a *pin-drop* silence. Everybody turned and looked at him, then looked at each other, then looked at all the Angels and started talking at once.

But I thought, *if you were dead you would be like a ghost and just float around…*I thought *if you were dead, you would not have the same body. I was really smashed up in my accident and yet I am fine; I don't get it.* The facilitator looked at all the people and said, *dear souls, you are in Heaven.* Boy, you could have knocked me over with a feather! Oh, I must have turned 4 shades of white, I was so shocked. I was thinking, *gosh, my death was fairly easy compared to everyone else's. I just went to sleep!* The Angel said, *yes, we helped your soul to release while you were asleep. It is one of the easiest and most painless ways to cross.* We said, *we did not see any tunnel.* He said, *you do not remember that. Some of you* *went through the tunnel and others did not. But you all came to the Care Center. You see, when people arrive in Heaven, they are placed with people who are kind of—we'll put it this way—people who are on the same wavelength. Some can be rich and some can be poor, but everyone is more or less at the same level. I don't mean emotional level, but spiritual growth level—consciousness growth. So as you look around you,* the facilitator continues, *you are all about on the same level. You could say in this room that none of you believed you were dead. And yet, there are highly educated people among you and some people who never finished high school.*

So with that, Thief-man continues, *that was my awakening to being dead. It was a shock-eroo, I must tell you. I understand there will be a question and answer period, so I am open to any questions you wish to ask me.*

Questions (Q) and Answers (A)

Q: One of the questions I usually ask is how old were you when you died? Do you remember that?

A: *Oh yes, I was in my twenties because I had just graduated from college and had traveled a bit, so I was 27.*

Q: How long has it been since you have had a body?

A: *Do you mean born again, reincarnated? Yes. I am not sure.*

Q: What form do you have now?

A: *I have the body I came in; I am healed.*

Q: In your life's review, did you find out what your purpose in that lifetime was? What the purpose was in all of those history classes you took and so forth?

A: *Hmm, I had not thought of that. I don't really know.*

Q: Did you finish your contract? You know, each time a person takes a body, there is a contract.

A: *I think I must have because I died.*

Q: Do you believe in reincarnation?

A: *I didn't at the time, but I do now because I know so many people seem to be going back again.*

Q: When you go back, will you have a new vocation?

A: *Well, I never had one in that lifetime, so yes. When I am in college, I've got to pick something else for when I get out—you know, like a lawyer. At least you can be a lawyer to somebody. But with a history major, it is sort of like, what do I do with it? You can teach it, but then in order to teach it, you have to take more classes in order to learn how to teach. So that's not good.*

Q: What was your biggest regret after you had found out you had died?

A: *The biggest regret was I never had a family of my own. I never married or had children. I had some girlfriends, but nothing permanent.*

Q: So what are you being retrained about now—being taught what you could change?

A: *Actually, all sorts of things. Since I am interested in history, I wanted to know about some of the religions of course—Jesus and all of that. So I had to work with some of my belief systems, because when I had a body, I knew I had a choice—if you didn't, you know, have what is called a good life—you would go to Hell. I know that's been changed, for Hell is my own choice in my own head. So we learned about that.*

I learned about love. Everything is love here. You feel love; you know love. They teach it. There are classes. They teach about love and the depth of love, the different ways people on Earth love—you know, they possess; or they control; or they don't love very deeply and stuff like that. That was very interesting to me since I had no family. I thought when I go back, I can then have a family. I can love my wife and I can love my kids at a deep level and try not to possess them and stuff like that.

Q: Have you met with any past relatives who are on your side?

A: *Oh, there are lots of people, but I don't know them. Remember I died when I was only 27, so there are a lot of past relatives. They come up and say they were my Aunt so-and-so or my Uncle so-and-so or my father in a past life, but it doesn't make any sense to me. I just try to be nice.*

Q: Have you met any of the Ascended Masters?

A: *I don't know what you mean by Ascended or Masters, but there are what I call* great Beings *who have a beautiful Light. That's how I knew who you were because your Light is so bright.* Thank you.

Q: You say you just woke up in the Caring Center, so you have not seen pearly gates, streets paved with gold?

A: *No I haven't seen any of that. I don't even know if there is that. I keep forgetting to ask any of the others if they saw that or not.*

Q: Did you attend your funeral or memorial and if so, how did you do that?

A: *Actually, my Angel…I think it was in a dream when I was in the Care Center. I had a dream where I went to this funeral. So maybe I was actually there; I don't know. People were bawling and my college friends, buddies, all looked kind of sad, which kind of amused me for they used to tease me so much; anyway…I didn't stay very long; you know how those things go.*

Q: Just a few more questions here. Are you alright with that?

A: *Yes, I am having a great time.*

Q: Tell me the procedure for coming to me. How far into my aura are you?

A: *The great Being told me you were writing a book and would I come and tell you about my death process. He said to just come and talk to you. He said I would know how close to you to go because I would not be able to get any closer.* (The Ring-Pass-Not) *And that was true; I could come just so far and that was it.*

Q: Since you have been in Heaven, what are your activities? What else have you done except view your life review and meet with your group?

A: *Well, I am still traveling. I like that one can just hop on a bus or on a train. I just found out the other day that you could take a trip by airplane. I did not know that this place was so big. I thought it was just the size of a large city or something. Now I am finding out it is like a state, or country, or a group of countries—maybe more than that. I don't know—maybe like a star. It's huge. I don't think I could ever see the whole thing. I understand there are places we can go to and other places we can't, because you have to be evolved to a certain depth, or whatever they call it—dimension, I guess—in order to get there. It would be like when you are on Earth trying to climb Mt. Everest. If you have never climbed before, you certainly aren't going to reach the top. Maybe you can go only a little way and that is as high as you can go. That's kind of what it's like here—climbing Mt. Everest. Those Masters you've been speaking of, I'm sure they've been to the top, but that's all I know about it.*

Q: So have you seen God and what is called on Earth, the *Judgment Seat,* and all of that?

A: *No, and that has always kind of puzzled me because we, of course, were taught on Earth in religion that we better be good, for when we go to stand before God, he is going to judge us. That has not happened, so I don't know if it's going to happen or happen later or never happen; I don't know. There's lots I don't know. We can always go to that facilitator, for we still meet in that group. My Guardian Angel seems to know a lot. I can always go to him also.*

Q: We are coming to the end of our interview now. Are there any questions you would like to ask me—anything at all?

A: *Well, how do you get to be where you can have dead people come to you?*

When you are on Earth, there are people who have trained themselves to talk telepathically, which means mental-to-mental with people. When they hear them, it is called channeling and they are talking back and forth. So you learn to channel. I have learned that, and in that way, I am able to talk with you. However, there are all different types of mediums—channels—and I channel mostly the Masters for my books. But there are people who just channel dead people who come all the time to them and talk to them. (*Long Island Medium*). But I have invited the people who come to me. Does that answer your question?

Yes, and I thank you for that. I always thought stuff of that nature was of woo-woo land, but I see now that you have a great purpose in this, and you use the information and you write books with it which can be very enlightening for people. So I am excited that my story will be in one of your books; I thank you for that.

You are most welcome. We have come to the end of our interview, unless you wish to say anything more to me.

No, I cannot think of anything else, but thank you so much! This has been the greatest trip I have been on. It has been so much fun. Wait until I tell the gang. I thank you so much.

You are welcome (*smile*), and I am honored that you came and told me and the readers about your experience. I have enjoyed it, and they will enjoy reading about it. With that, I say thank you again, I wish you all the best for your next lifetime and may God give you many blessings.

Thank you, thank you!

You are welcome. Bye for now.

Bye.

Alright, dear one. The purpose of that chapter was to show the readers that not everyone knows he or she is dead. There are all types of experiences by the time one reaches Heaven.

Yes, what surprised me is not everyone goes through the tunnel.

Yes, that is true, dear one. You can bypass that.

Thank you, Sananda. We did Chapter 4!

Yes, you did. Until we meet again, dear one. Love from my heart, I Am Sananda.

Thank you, Sananda; love from my heart to yours. Namaste!

8:20 AM

5 DOCTOR-MAN

03-08-15 *Good morning, dear one; you are all set to go, I see.* Yes, Lord; I wanted to ask you in what dimension am I meeting all of these Beings. Is it always the same dimension?

Yes, dear one; you are meeting them in the fifth dimension.

Alright, thank you.

Now, this will be our fifth chapter with the code name of Doctor-man. At the end I will discuss my reason for choosing him to represent a group dynamic.

Hello, I don't know what I am supposed to be doing here. *Alright, greetings, thank you for coming. Did you get more or less instructed as to what is going on?* Kind of, but I am not real sure. *You are being given a code name of* Doctor-man. *It does not mean that was who you were in that past life. We are going through the nursery rhymes, and each one who comes to be interviewed has a code name. You have been instructed not to give out personal names and so forth because of all the legal ramifications that could ensue. So are you ready to give us your story?*

Yes, I was a young man, and there is that term, *not dry behind the ears.* I think that was me. You know, I have had the life's review on those screens. I could see more of who I was in that lifetime—not always a pleasant thing to view, but it certainly answered a lot of questions for me. I will say that I was arrogant and thought I knew it all. My family was just of moderate income—we'll say *middleclass*. I had the usual upbringing—went to school, finished high school, did one year in college—then I got into trouble.

Of course, in that day and age, not too long ago, the trouble was always alcohol or drugs or both. So I started drinking too much and getting in with a rowdy crowd, not doing my homework. And I flunked out of college.

Then my parents, of course, did not have the money to keep sending me to college if there was not graduation at the end. They kind of made an ultimatum: we'll give you three months of free room and board and then you will need to move out because you need to find you own life. We are not going to raise a son who will be just a lush and take a free ride.

Of course, at that time I hated them, but after my review, I realized that was the best thing they could have done for me. Anyway, back to that time, I did a lot of swearing and four letter words and said, *well f... you*. I thought that but did not dare say it out loud. *I am not going to stay here. I'll throw some things in a suitcase and go live with my friend* (I'll call him *Johnny*). As it turned out he wasn't all that helpful either. He didn't pay his bills; his rent was due.

I had no money. Everybody was drinking. When they started stealing this and that and then selling it in order to get money, there was that nagging thought in the back of my head that said, *if I stay around here I am going to get in big trouble and I don't want to go to jail. I am not going to do this and be the scape-goat for all of these losers.* So again I just packed up my bag and left.

I did not know where I was going. My parents had given me a little bit of *walking-out* money—fifty dollars. Of course, fifty dollars seemed like quite a bit of money back then, but I am soon finding out that if I stuck around with what I used to call *friends*, I would not have anything left. They were like hmm, gosh... Anyone who had money was fair game. You were expected to pay for all the liquor and any food until that was gone. Then they turned to someone else, or they brought a new person into the group.

They were always trying to find a rich guy that they could kind of flam-boozle and just kind of leach off of him. So thank God I saw the writing on the wall and got out of there. I just packed up my suitcase and said, *I want to go see the world, you guys. I hope you have a good life.* And I walked out.

I must say that at that time—I must have been 19 or 20 or something like that—at that age to have enough sense to realize I was going down a slippery slope real fast and to get out was brave of me. So I pat myself on my back on that.

Now I get to the part where I am not very proud of what happened next. Apparently, I was a good-looking guy and with my arrogance, I could strut along. The girls kind of fell over me. Sure enough, I picked a rich one. I wasn't going to lock myself up with someone who could not pay my bills. I had already played that with my so-called buddies, so I kind of looked around. We sparked it right off. I guess you could say it was from the times before. (I am learning now we had lives together before. You see, I am learning about past lives and reincarnation, so obviously we had a connection there.)

So I kind of went after her, although she did not know that. She was kind of one of these spoiled girls. They showered her with everything. She had a beautiful convertible. In those days if you had a convertible, you were really in the in-crowd. She had this gorgeous convertible. It was blue. She let me drive it, and I felt like a king when I drove that convertible. I said right from the beginning I was going to have this woman and have that car. And that's what happened.

I don't know why her parents put up with me. I guess I was a very smooth talker and had had some college, so they did not see me as a total loser. Her father gave me a job in his company. I was smart enough to be able to do the work that was assigned to me, although I was not all that eager for it. It was some type of business I had no interest in. I did that for a while.

Then the babies started coming. While I was quite proud as a peacock that I had a son, when it came to a daughter and then another son, another son, another daughter, I said, *whoa, this is too much; I've got to get out of here.* See, I loved this woman as much as I could; I loved my kids as much as I could, but I found at times they all were just kind of a drag on me. (Of course, in my review I realized this was an immature part of me.) I am getting ahead of my story.

So what did I do? I walked out! I made up some excuse, packed my bags, said I had to travel on some business and kissed them all goodbye. My wife just thought it was a business trip and off I went. I never looked back, which I am not too proud of.

I caught a boat; I can't say it was a big magnificent ship, because I did not want to spend my money on that. So I guess it was a freighter I hopped. I wasn't about to fly, because I did not think airplanes were all that trustworthy. I went of all places—I went to Australia. The Australians for some reason were fascinated by Americans. I could play that role, you see—kind of a *playboy*, so to speak. I made up stories how I had lost my money and was over there seeking my fortune.

So I did that. Again I had the women running after me, but I had already been in that fix. I was still married so I did not want to tell them that. I was kind of foot loose and fancy free. Everybody was wining and dining me. Life was good. I really was enjoying it.

Oh man, and then it happened. I swear. It seems as if bad luck just follows me. You know, getting in the wrong crowd in college. That was such bad luck. Then my parents kicking me out of the house… That was bad luck. Then my wife having all of those kids. My God! To me that was bad luck. Now here I am; I thought I was going to get away from it all. Here I am in Australia and bad luck happened again!

You aren't going to believe this. (*Long sigh.*) You see there are places in Australia that are still very primitive, the *Outback*. I went into the Outback, and I went thinking I would just, you know, have a look-see, come back, and be the playboy again. I did not realize just how huge Australia was. It is the size of the United States. It's just huge. Of course, the coasts are inhabited, but as you left them and went into the Outback, there is nobody around except the Aborigines. I wasn't about to hook up with them.

So here I am driving an old car. I had gassed up and intended to drive just a little way and maybe I would meet some new people. I was always looking for an adventure. But as I said, it seemed that bad luck always followed me. I know in the review that's called being the *victim*. But, you see, I did not know that then. But as I look back, I was the victim of everything. I did not know about karma and all of that stuff. However, as I look back I see now these were karmic pieces I was playing out.

Here I am driving what you would call a *jalopy*, bumping along in the Outback where there are really no roads, but ruts, you know. When the rains came and it was all mud, you'd (*carts and trucks*) make these grooves and then they would dry and become ruts. So I was bouncing along these ruts not paying much attention when the car started of sputtering *put-put-put* and stopped! I exclaimed, *oh, Christ*! I was out of gas. Now, I did not know what I was going to do.

It was hotter than Hades. I climbed out and had my hat on. (You know those hats that have these little corks that are strung all along the rim, so that every time you swing your head the corks would swing too and keep the flies from landing on your face—it's sheep country and man, do they have flies in Australia—at least they did then.)

I climb out of the car and the little corks are swinging like crazy to keep the flies off me. I look around and the sun is right over my head. I'm sweating up a storm and I am just thinking, *oh, my God; what am I going to do now?* Well, I was not a praying man, and since I have never asked God for anything, I did not quite know how to approach this situation. I kind of just said, *well, if there is a God, come and help me 'cause my bad luck is following right behind me!*

Since my review, we were taught you aren't going to solve anything as long as you're in victim-mode. But I did not know that then. I was the victim to everything that happened to me. I did not know what to do. My car had a running-board—they had running-boards then. My car was just a jalopy. I did not think to bring an extra can of gas, and I wasn't focused on food all that much. I always watched my physical appearance. As I've said, I was tall and handsome, and I did not want to be fat with a paunch like so many men get. I guess you could say that was my prime-of-life.

I started to get afraid. The sun was beating down on me, so I had to crawl back into the car. But, of course, it was like crawling back into an oven. I had all the windows down, and it was better than having the sun scorching me and the corks flying all around to keep the flies off my face. Of course, they came into the car. I remember sort of collapsing on top of the steering wheel and sort of crying out, *Jesus, what am I going to do? Jesus, it's hot; Jesus, these damn flies.*

I took a few breaths; I was tired. I didn't realize it, but I had put my head back on the head rest of the seat and the next thing I knew, I had gone to sleep. I just was exhausted and even in that heat, I just went to sleep.

When I awoke, it was dark. It took me a while to get my bearings until it dawned on me, *oh crap*! Yep, right in the Outback—no food, no water, no gas, no lights. I did have a flashlight. I reached under the seat and brought that out, so I had some light. But I did not leave it on 'cause then the mosquitoes would just come in and attack me. So I couldn't really use that. I did not know what to do. I had no place to go. I was so thirsty. I just didn't know what to do.

Then I felt myself get a little… I guess I was getting a bit delirious. I said again, *I just have to get out of here,* and against any better judgment, I left the flashlight in the car and climbed out and started walking. Of course, I got even more totally lost!

I came to an area that was kind of all (*brambly*) shrub, thorny and just like a barrier. I had no knife, so I just got all entangled in that. By this time I am getting hysterical. I started screaming, *help; help; get me out of here*! There was just dead silence.

I felt myself kind of fainting because, of course, I had had nothing to eat nor to drink. I knew I was dehydrated, so I fainted. I just sort of hung there in all the entanglement of the thorny bush. I thought of all my bad luck, and it was never my fault that all this stuff happened to me. It was always someone else's fault—just my bad luck that was following me. I was damning everything as I lost consciousness.

I remember kind of dreaming as I was zooming through this tunnel. Everything was black; there was a light at the end of this tunnel. I had read about this before. I was very curious about it all but had no power to stop myself. I just zoomed through the tunnel whether I wanted to or not. It was like being… I can't think of the word. It is like you were exploded out from a cannon, and you go through this tunnel until you get to the end of it. And, of course, there was the light, and I am looking around and standing up again.

I noticed all these scratch marks on me. There was a man standing by me. I am saying, *Jesus* (swearing again), *can you help me? I am so thirsty; do you have any water on you?* He handed me a flask of water. I gulped that down and then said, *oh, thank you; I don't know what happened, but if I had stayed out there much longer, I would have bit the dust; that would have been it! Thanks a lot.*

Now, can you help me here? My car is out there some place in the Outback and I've got to get back through that tunnel. Is that a train; do I get on a train and go back out? Can someone help me find my car? Do you know of anybody who can help me with all of that?

The man just kind of smiled and said, *sir, why don't you come with me first and we will take care of your cuts and mosquito bites and things like that and get you rested a little bit. Then I will see what I can do.*

He took me to this building; it was huge. I still hadn't wised up. He took me to a very pleasant room and told me to take my clothes off, for they were all dusty and kind of bloody. *You can lie down between these clean sheets and have a little snooze here.*

I did as I was told. I noted that I was just so tired and it was nice to have someone look after me. I guess I fell asleep. When I awoke, I noticed all the scratches and cuts on my arms and hands and face were all healed; they were gone! I said to the man who was still there, *goodness sake.* (Actually, I said *hot damn!*) *This place really does heal you.* He said, *yes, it's the Care Center.* I said, *oh, where are we? Where is this Care Center?* He said, *you don't know yet?* I said, *no.* He said, *this is Heaven.*

I said, *boy, I'll say it's Heaven; you ought to see it out there! But no, really. Where is this place? I did not know Australia had such a place here.* He said, *come sir; I want to show you something.*

He led me and pretty soon I was standing in front of these screens. There was my whole life. I thought, *this is strange,* and then I got caught up into watching. The weird thing of it was I could see everything, feel everything—kind of like both sides of the fence. I could see what I did and at the same time feel what they were feeling about it. It was really kind of neat until I got to the parts where the other person was feeling a lot of anguish and pain, and I started seeing how my actions had hurt so many people. I was surprised because I had not known how I had let my parents down by drinking away their money in college. The best thing they had done for me was to kick me out, although it was done in a loving way, which I had not realized.

Then I met my lovely wife who <u>really</u> loved me and gave me those children who I did not appreciate. So it (*my life's story*) went on and on. I saw myself coming to Australia just trying to take from everyone; my journey to the Outback, to just explore I thought, and getting trapped in the thorny bush. I actually saw myself die. That was a real shock. I said, *holy shit, I really am dead. I really <u>am</u> dead!* Hmm, and everything I had heard about Heaven is certainly true so far. You don't feel dead. You feel well, in fact you feel better than you did when you were alive.

I started looking, observing more around me and noticed that everyone had robes on including myself. I was brought to this room where there were a whole bunch of people there—maybe 50 people. They all had on different colored robes. They were all telling their stories.

There was a teacher who we called a *facilitator* who led us along. We started talking about our different belief systems. I started really thinking about myself and not being all that proud about the things I had done in my lifetime. While I had not particularly believed in reincarnation, I knew now that that was a very probable event that will happen in my lifetime. I will go back; I have to go back. Look at all the karma I accrued. When you are the victim throughout your whole life, don't you think that is creating karma—you know, cause and effect? *What you cause someone, you will be the effect of.*

So when I came here to you (*Author*), I was told that after I told my story, there would be a series of questions that I am to give answers to the best of my ability and stuff like that. I have now told you my story, so I turn it over to you and what you would like to say about it.

Thank you and yes, there will be a question and answer period. There will be little pauses as I read through my list in order to not have the same questions for everybody.

Questions (Q) and Answers (A)

Q: Have you or anyone in the group that you are with... (I assume you are in the same group as when you first got there?)

A: *Yes, we've decided to stay together—sort of like-minds.*

Q: Do any of you ever return to people on Earth, not that you are reincarnated, but you just go to visit them? Maybe some people play tricks on them—knock books off of shelves, stop clocks—or something like that? Do any of you return and do that?

A: *You know that is one of the things the facilitator talked about. The only time we return is when we have visited our funeral, which reminds me I had a dream... I did go back! I saw everybody. There was Mom and Dad, my wife, and all the kids and yeah, I did go back. Of course, everybody was crying and I tried to make myself known. Nobody sees or hears me; they're all thinking I'm dead, and I am trying to tell them I'm right here. No one is paying attention. They are just kind of caught up in the moment of mourning my life. I remember thinking to myself isn't it too bad that people can't see through this—whatever it is—this mist and see you are alive. In fact, you are in better shape than when you were on Earth. You know so much more now and you are a better person. It's too bad that they don't see that at that time.*

So anyway, I did go visit, but that is not what you mean. You mean did I kind of go back like a ghost would go back? Well, that is one way to put it, but you know there have been people who return to their loved ones or to their business partners and try to make themselves known again. And try to stick around and try to get the person's attention by maybe displacing things. It never seems to work, so I was just curious if anyone in your group had done that?

I don't know about the others; I just know that I have not. The facilitator did say that that was not desirable. We are not ghosts. That is kind of a lower vibrational acting and it was not growth. Everything seems to be growth oriented. You do this, and it is like climbing a ladder. You are going higher. But if you do such and such, then you are not climbing that ladder.

That's the way they talk about people who go back and try to get someone to feel them or hear them or something like that. You know, you learn many things while you are here in Heaven. Little is constant; there is always change. Some things like the Caring Center and the Review screens and the Counseling Groups are all constants. But everything else changes: some people eat, others don't; some people sleep, others don't; some people travel, others don't. It is very enlightening to note that. Thank you. I want to get back to some of the basic questions.

Q: How old were you when you died?

A: *Well, let's see. I was married for around 5 years, I guess, so I would have been in my mid-twenties then. Then I left and went to Australia and kind of screwed around and I was there 2-3 years, I guess. You know time… There is no time up here, so I can only say that time is kind of fleeting, but I was probably in my early thirties.*

Q: So how long has it been since you have had a body?

A: *I don't quite understand.*

Q: I mean have you reincarnated? Are you still in a body-form?

A: *Oh, I am in a body-form; I have the same body that I had when I came* (to Heaven). *I like that body; it is a very handsome body. The only thing is it does like alcohol. Of course, there is no alcohol here and that has put me on the wagon fast. I know I will have to go back, and I want to take this body with me.*

Q: What was your purpose in that lifetime? You know that everyone when born into a body has a purpose. There is a contract.

A: *Gosh, that's a good one, but you know—I can't say for sure, but after seeing my review—I would say my purpose was to be kinder to people and not always be the victim to everything. I was the victim to so much. They have what they call the* Law of Attraction. *They were teaching that when I was a victim to so much, I was just attracting all of that to happen to me. That need not have happened. I could have had my little jaunt to the Outback but maybe I would have had a companion or had extra gas and food and water in the car—all that kind of stuff. But I didn't, so I was just sort of a victim to all of that. I would say that was my purpose.*

Q: Did you finish your contract?

A*: I am not real sure on that one either. Maybe whoever does this just decided I had had enough bad luck and took me to Heaven.*

Q: When you return, will you have a new vocation?

A: *Well, I'll certainly have to do something, won't I? I just can't go to college and not do anything. I know I will go to college because I am smart. But I have to decide to do something, won't I?*

Q: So what is your biggest regret?

A: *Well, I am not sure I regret anything because I have learned so much from all of it. I am sorry I have hurt people. I think you could say my biggest regret was my belief system, my attitude of always being the victim. Boy, when people read your book and just understand that one—**stay out of victim-hood**! That's a biggie.*

Q: So what are you being retrained about now?

A: *That is sort of like being re-taught, isn't it? Yes. Well, a great deal of it is we use the* Law of Attraction *and not to be the victim to everything and how you attract that negativity to you. I am being retrained about all of that.*

Q: Have you met past relatives?

A: *There are some here—you meet them, but I have not paid all that much attention to them. I know some guys are all caught up in the fact they are meeting a past wife or something like that, but I did not have anything like that. Mine were just kind of relatives I grew up with but did not pay that much attention to.*

Q: Have you met any of the Ascended Masters like Jesus? Or whatever your religion was?

A: *I didn't have a religion, per se. I believed in God. I knew there was a Jesus, but I didn't go to church. You know during the different times like Christmas and everyone talked about Jesus and you went to church and sung the hymns and stuff like that, but that wasn't a strict belief for me. It was like going to the movies. I just enjoyed it. So as far as the Ascended Masters and meeting Jesus, I can't say that I have. I know when one of them is visiting for there is this great Light and everyone is running to it, but I haven't had one stop and say,* hey Joe, how are you doing, *or something like that. (Of course, that is not my real name, but you know what I mean.)* Yes.

Q: So you haven't seen pearly gates and streets paved with gold?

A: *No, they've talked about that and that is all people's imagination. That is not true.*

Q: While you are in Heaven are you doing a particular job that has a title?

A: *Hmm, I know what you mean. Some people can work in the Archives and places like that, but no, I am sort of just going to my group and going to the dining hall. I pretty much just do what I want to do.*

Q: Have you done any exploring? You know Heaven is a very large area.

A: *No, I think the fact I went exploring while in Australia and ended up killing myself kind of put a damper on anything like that. I pretty well stay what we say is close to Home.*

Q: What are your living arrangements?

A: *Oh, some of the other guys and I kind of live, I don't know what it's called—in a dormitory or apartment or what. Actually it's kind of a house. There is a group of us all living in this house. I know what it reminds me of—a fraternity house. That's what it's like.*

Q: Did you build that or was there just one there that you all moved into? How is that done?

A: *Oh, we were assigned to this. There was just a group of us that signed up, and we were just sent there. It is a very nice house! They have quite a few of these—almost like Fraternity Row* (like in college).

Q: So you still eat the food and all of that?

A: *Yes. I must admit the fact that I did not have any food for so long a time, I do not want to be without food or water.*

Q: We have come to the end of our interview. Is there anything you wish to say to me?

A: *No, just to thank you; it's been a great experience, and I have had a lot of fun. I just thank you. Your energy field is very brilliant.*

I thank you also. It was an honor for me to have you come and tell your story. I thank you very much. Now we will say goodbye.

Goodbye, thank you again.

You are most welcome. The interview is finished.

Ok, Sananda.

Can you guess the theme of that person?

Yes, not to be a victim.

Exactly. It always kind of amazes us as to how many people still play the victim. They die and they are a victim. They do not see the role they play in their story. Alright, dear one, you have lots to type up. I know it may be a little difficult this week for you but just know when you are ready to sit, I will be there also.

Thank you, Sananda.

You are welcome, dear heart. Over and out!

Thank you, my love to you. 8:25 AM

6 LAWYER-MAN

O 3-12-15 Good morning, precious one; all set to work once again (7:05 AM). *Yes, Lord. (It was at this time that I did not see that the red record button was not fully engaged. Therefore, the first third of Lawyer-man's story was not recorded. I will paraphrase what he said up to where the machine started to record again. Thankfully, I recorded the rest of his story successfully.)*

Lawyer-man was the only son of a well-to-do family. He was catered to in every way. His father saw to it that he entered an Ivy League college. He graduated but with no particular vocation he wanted to pursue. He decided to travel.

He did not want to go to a country where he would get "down and dirty." He chose the Scandinavian countries. He hired a guide and decided to climb a mountain and then ski back down. His guide warned him to stay on the "beaten path," for the avalanches came without notice and buried you in a matter of minutes.

He climbed for a while and then decided to change pace and ski back down. His guide warned him again to be careful. He snapped on his skis and enjoyed the feeling of flying down the steep slope. He noticed new snow on the side of the trail and in a split second veered off course just a bit. He thought just a foot over would not make a difference.

Then he heard his guide yelling, Avalanche! *With a quick glance backward, he saw this mountainous wave of snow bearing down on him. He hoped he could out-run it, but he was engulfed in the snow before he could even finish his thought. He heard this roar and turned his head into his armpit in order to give him a small pocket of air before he was completely buried.*

(The tape picks up the narrative.) I knew I was losing consciousness, for there was a roaring in my ears and I knew I was going to black out. That was the last I remembered. We'll say the last I remembered of that lifetime. Snuffed out in the prime of life for a stupid, stupid mistake!

Well, my guide had escaped the avalanche, so he got busy—he had these kind of radio things on him—and called for help. All he could tell them was an area where he thought I was. My skis were not sticking out of the top of the snow, so all my guide could say was he was in there someplace, pointing to a large area some distance from him. Therefore, it was quite a while before they found me. If they found the skis, they were no longer on my feet. They (*rescuers*) dug around and finally found my body.

I do not know how long I laid there unconscious, but the next thing I knew I was here in Heaven. I don't know how I got here. There was no tunnel; there was nothing. It seems like one minute I am skiing down the slopes and the next minute I am buried. There was a man with me, thank God, for I was disoriented.

He said, *come, sir, let me take you to the Care Center. You have many bruises that need attending to.* Well, I was so out of it; I did not quite know where I was, who I was, what he was. I just followed him like a dog. *Come with me puppy; that a-boy, come on.* Then he took me to this pleasant looking room, told me to take off my wet clothes and boots and climb into bed. I followed his instructions without trying to figure out what was going on. I just collapsed into bed and the next thing I knew, I went to sleep.

When I awoke, that's when I started interrogating him. I awoke feeling very refreshed—no longer any bruises on me. They brought me a cup of really good tea. They asked if I wanted to have anything to eat. I said I would love to have a piece of toast or something like that. They brought me a slice of toast; it had some delicious honey on it. I had that and my tea.

All the time I am eating and drinking, I am asking this man all these questions. *Ok, now tell me what happened. How did you get me here? What is this place; is this kind of a healing chateau? I don't remember seeing it.* I did not have a <u>c-lue</u> where I was. Of course, I asked the man who he was and he said, *I am your Guardian Angel.* I said, *yeah, I sure needed one.*

I did not take him verbatim. He just let my remark slide. One thing I have learned is they...(I'll say *they* because there were several Angels.)... they do not press you into trying to understand—press you to become more oriented. They just leave it up to you as a gradual introduction, we'll say. So when I made remarks of *yeah, right,* or things of that nature, the man just was not defensive in any way. He just seemed to be a really nice guy. I felt that he really liked me, although I don't see how he could particularly know me, but he was just a nice guy. When I asked him, *how long have you been here?* He replied, *oh, I have been here a long time.* Then I said, *well, do you work here?* He said, *yes, you could say that.*

It seemed as if you never got a definitive answer from him, but it was always just enough to lead you on to the next question. Then he said, *alright sir, now that you have had your tea and crumpets,* meaning the toast of course, *follow me; I want to take you to another building.*

I followed and noticed how extraordinarily huge these building were. The grounds were magnificent and the grass and flowers…*God, where am I? This place is extraordinary.* It was a gardener's dream—just spectacular!

So we went to this other building, and it seemed to be the one with a lot of computers and huge screens. People were in the room. Some were standing; some were sitting; some were crying as they looked at these screens. I thought, *boy, they must be watching different movies.* You know maybe someone has this one movie that is very moving for him and he is crying. Another one just is sitting there stunned. I did not get it. It seemed as if this was a huge movie house, or something like that, although it was not dark in there.

My man took me to this huge screen that started playing immediately. I could hear the sound. (You could hear yours, but you could not hear anyone else's sound. I was next to this one guy. It was like he was in the next room. You could not hear his movie; I could just hear my own.) I was led to my screen and had a comfortable chair to sit in. The movie had already started. I exclaimed, *oh, it has already started!* He just smiled at me and said, *yes.* So I looked and was astonished because…*Why, that's me! Oh, my gosh, this is me; you have movies of my family. Oh, look at my mother; isn't she beautiful? And my father… Look at all the toys I had; ah, I had forgotten that; how great. Oh, look at them; they really loved me.*

Oh-oh, I am throwing a temper tantrum here. Hmm, who is that? Oh, that was our maid. Uh, I was kind of mean to her. She would let me have my temper tantrum and just let me scream. That would just get me madder.

Here I am…Oh, this is high school. Oh, look at that. There's my puppy. Oh, I loved that dog! I went on and on like that and I still had no clue.

I thought someone had taken movies of me and was just showing me this. You see I was not around people who had esoteric knowledge, or who talked about metaphysics or anything like that. I had no clue of any of this stuff.

I don't think I had ever heard of a *life's review*. Nobody talked about death or what happens afterwards or anything like that. It was just a given that I and everybody in the family would go to Heaven. It was not even a thought that there would be a Hell. We did not think like that. When I come to think about it, we had church and we kids went to church, but I don't remember talking about the afterlife.

In the meantime, as I sat there viewing my life—we'll say my *short life*—the man just kept standing there by my chair. When I got to the avalanche, I just got terrified, reliving it all again. I saw where I was completely covered (*by snow*) and feeling again where I could not breathe—just blacking out. It was as though someone had written on the screen *THE END*. I was waiting for the lights to come back on. *OK, that's the end*. I just sat there kind of stunned. I said to the man by me, *well, that's an interesting movie, but if anyone tries to sell it, they aren't going to make much money on that one!*

I had girlfriends and fiddled around but didn't have steamy sex and all of that you see in other movies. Then the man standing by me said, *alright sir, we are going to now go to another area.* He led me to this room that had quite a few people in it. I did not count them one by one, but maybe 40-50 people in it. Everybody was kind of paired up and talking to each other. I found a chair and sat down and waited to see *ok, what else is going to happen now*? I had had my nap, had had my tea, seen a movie; now what?

Pretty soon, a man entered the room and everybody just sort of stopped talking. The man introduced himself and said he was the facilitator of this group. (And oh, by the way, we were all in these comfortable robes, which I found was kind of unusual. Each one had different colors and mine was blue, which I learned symbolized peace. Well, I sure needed that at this point—to get smothered in an avalanche, you need a little peace afterwards.)

We all sat there and waited for the facilitator to make his statement. He started talking about our life reviews. I thought, *oh, so that's what you call it—my moving picture was a life review. Yeah, it was.* Then he asked, *are there any of you who are not quite sure where you are yet?* Some hands shot up, including mine. He nodded at me and I said, *yes, I don't know where I am, for I had passed out. Next thing I knew, I was here feeling rested, being given tea and toast, then saw this movie of my life. Now here I am sitting here with all these guys in different colored robes. I am not quite sure what's going on.*

He asked each one of us (*the same question*) and then launched into his topic of Heaven—*this is what is known as Heaven. Some call it Nirvana, but for clarity, we will just refer to it as* Heaven. Then we had to wait for the surprise to sink in and subside. There were many exclamations: *you've got to be kidding! I always heard of this place but did not know it is actually here* (that it exists)*; I still don't believe it.*

That's kind of where it's at. When this Great Being came to me and asked if I would tell my story, and of course I agreed, he brought me to you and said you would have some questions and stuff.

Thank you for your story, and yes, I do have what is called Q and A types of questions for you to answer if you don't mind. They are very similar to what I have asked the others and I hope the questions will be fine for you also.

Questions (Q) and Answers (A)

Q: *What form are you in now? You have told me and the readers of being in your discussion room. I assume that has continued for a while?*

A: Yes, we go and meet every day. I have noticed that some no longer meet with us. It is kind of shrinking. As to what form I have, I have the one I arrived in. Is that what you mean? *Yes. After you have been there a while, you can move up the ladder, so to speak, and no longer need a body. You are just in Spirit energy.* Oh, maybe that is what happened to the others. All of us still have the body we arrived in. *Alright.*

Q: *Another question some have asked is are you with your soul group or is it still with the group that all kind of died around the same time?*

A: Our facilitator told us that each of us belonged to a particular soul group and when the time was right, we would be meeting that group. But I have not met mine yet.

Q: *So what was your purpose in that lifetime?*

A: *That's a good one* (question*). What would be the purpose of someone being born and given everything and then dying in an avalanche? I don't know; it has not been discussed, and I am not sure what my purpose was, or should say is.*

Q: Do you have any particular regrets?

A: *Ye-ah; I regret having died so soon. Look at everything I had ahead of me. I didn't marry; I didn't have a family. I regret that. Then after my life's review, I regret I wasn't more appreciative of what my family had provided for me and how they loved me. I didn't appreciate all of that, obviously.*

Q: Will you reincarnate again?

A: *Well, do you mean go back and live that same life over again? I don't quite understand.*

Q: Have you talked about reincarnation in your group?

A: *Yes, it was mentioned, but a lot of people don't want to go back to their life again. I can't say I blame them; I don't want to go back to that life again either. If you mean by reincarnate to go and have another life, well, yes, I would like to do that. I would like to have a longer life. I don't care if I look the same or not; I just want a longer life so I can have a family.*

Q: What would you have as a vocation? You were rather foot-loose and fancy-free in that life time. So what would be your training; what would you like to do?

A: *Well, it is obvious to me that I want to work with people; I want to, if I can in some way, give them a sense of purpose. It is such a waste to… Life is just so short; look at mine. Who would have thought I would die in an avalanche, for Pete's sake? I just want to give people a warning: life is short. You don't know when it is going to be snuffed out. Just do something that will give to others.*

Q: Now are you being retrained for anything in particular now—like a belief system or something like that?

A: *I can't say that I am being retrained in something. I observe what's going on with others and the discussions and I am learning, but I can't say I am being retrained.*

Q: Have you met any of the Great Beings—Ascended Masters?

A: *No. You see, I did not have any religion—that's not the way to say it. We went to church and did all that because it was expected, but I did not really feel compelled to talk to Jesus, if you put it in those words. I didn't learn any of that. So no, I have not met any of the Ascended Masters. I know that they come to visit, but I have not met any.*

Q: Did you attend your own funeral or memorial?

A: *I must have but do not recall actually being there. But when I was asleep, I had a dream that I was. My mother was so sweet. She was just sobbing away. You see, I was their only son. It was a shock. My mother just kept saying over and over,* my beautiful boy; I hope he wasn't afraid.

Q: In your group, did you discuss religions and things of that nature?

A: *Only as it came up with other people. So many of them were Catholic, and they were really into their religion. Everybody believed in God, so that was not the discussion. It was just like, well, they weren't—I guess you would call that part the retraining—those who were heavily into their religion. That was discussed because so much they were taught while on Earth was not real. We found out it was too controlling. Much of the religion is man-made and controlling us—you must do this and you must do that. We found out that that was not truth.*

Q: How long have you been in Heaven?

A: *Well, I guess it has been a long time. I just know I graduated around 1925 or something like that.*

Q: So what are your living conditions then? Do you have a buddy system or do you live by yourself? How is that set up? The readers want to know all they can.

A: *Actually, I have a little house. I found that I like to build things. Here in Heaven we soon learned that anything we thought would manifest. So I decided I was going to build a house. That is what I did. I manifested every piece of it. It is a nice little house. It is not pretentious. I had all of that as a kid. I just want comfort. I don't need to impress anybody. Nobody impresses anyone here in Heaven because when you look at something, we know that that is* that *person's manifestation. That is what* they *are wanting; that is what* they *believe. And at any moment, they could just say* whoosh *and it would just disappear.*

Now, I could go by their house and say whoosh *and it would still be there. That is because those were not* my *thoughts that build it. With my house there are many times when I was building it and did not like what manifested. I said* whoosh *and it disappeared so I could start over. So I ended up with just a nice little place—one bedroom and one bathroom so I could have my shower.*

Oh, that's another thing. There are no toilets because we do not seem to evacuate our food. It is assimilated in some way so that my body has no waste. I find that interesting—there are no wastes here. Hmm, I had not thought much about that until now.

So anyway, I have this nice little house. I did manifest a kitchen, but only because I liked the idea of going to the kitchen and getting ice from the ice machine. That can just all go whoosh, too, *if I want it to disappear. But I like it; it reminds me of a little of home. Oh, I shouldn't say home because this is Home. This is Home with a capital H and the one on Earth has a small "h." It's not really our home. Heaven is our Home.*

Q: Do you have a particular job in Heaven? After you manifested your Home, do you do something to keep occupied? What do you do?

A: *I am thinking how to put this. I do not have a job, per se. I like to travel, so I did a little traveling. They have buses and trains and things like that. I did some of that. They even have cars that you can use, but I did not like to check out a car, for I did not know where to go. I did not want to get lost. Whereas if you go by bus, train, or even a plane, at least you know whoever is driving it knows where he is going.*

You see, I don't quite know yet how to navigate around Heaven without getting lost. How would I find my house again and how would I find my group again—not my soul group, for I have not met them yet, but the other group? I do have some friends and we are finding out that we had other lives together, which is a whole other subject. So I don't think I have a particular vocation I can tell you about, but I have traveled a bit.

I don't think people realize just how huge Heaven is. It is another world, you could say. Since I never saw all on the Earth world, I can't say I've seen all of Heaven either.

Q: Do you watch on the screens what is going on on Earth?

A: *Sometimes we do, but there is so much here you can do. I mean, why watch a concert on Earth, we'll say, when you can go to a concert here and the music is so up-lifting and you feel so healed afterwards? While on Earth, there are the crowds of people talking, etcetera. It is different up here. And no, there are no prize fights and NASCAR races and things like that here. Heaven is what will help you to evolve, we're told—beautiful ballets and concerts and things like that.*

Q: Do you still eat food, go to the dining hall, manifest your own food?

A: *It all depends on what mood I am in. Sometimes I go to the Dining Hall just for the comradery. Other times I feel like being solitary. Maybe I won't eat anything. I am gradually noticing I don't really need to eat food. I am only eating it out of habit, so to speak.*

Q: We are coming to the end of our interview. It has been an hour. Do you have anything you would like to ask me?

A: *That takes me by surprise; I wasn't expecting that. I think it must be kind of exciting for you to channel people and hear what they have to say.*

Yes, I enjoy that very much. It is actually a privilege.

I think when I get the courage to take another life, I would like to channel.

Q: You feel you are held back from Earth because you need more courage to do so?

A: *In some way, yes. I just don't know what stuff I would be getting back into. I am hesitant; I don't want to have nasty experiences. I just like the peacefulness. In fact I still wear my blue robes—not every place. I have some loose trousers and shirts; I designed those too. You know, you can do anything by thought. So I am not ready to give all that up and go back to Earth again. Some of my buddies have said there will come a time when I won't have a choice but will have to go back. I say to them, well, my choice is to not return right now.*

That is where I am. I am comfortable in Heaven. I don't want to go back yet. I don't want to get into a messy life. The facilitators tell you there will be a veil of forgetfulness so you will won't have those kinds of thoughts, but I have a feeling that life will be more difficult for me. I am shying away from that.

Q: I am saying again that our interview is drawing to a close, so I want to thank you for coming to me and telling me your story. I am greatly honored and wish you God's blessings on anything that you decide to do.

A: *Oh, thank you, I wasn't expecting that. That makes me feel good.*

Q: You are most welcome; our interview is now closed.

Alright, dear one. That was number 6.

Yes, died in an avalanche. Whew! To me that's a rough one, but I don't know why I would expect something different.

It is kind of amazing, isn't it, to hear of all the different ways someone has died?

Yes, and I feel I have only touched the tip of the ice berg.

Yes, dear one, that is true. Alright beloved, until we meet again. I Am Sananda. Thank you, Lord. Adieu.

7 MERCHANT-MAN

O3-15-15 *Good morning, precious one, another beautiful Sunday morning (8:05AM)* Yes, Lord. *Alright, dear one, we'll be bringing forth your Chapter 7 with the code name of* Merchant-Man. *This will be a bit different so that the readers can see there is a variety here. I will step aside now. He is eagerly awaiting, as they all are.*

Good morning to whoever is there.

Oh, I am so excited; thank you for having me come. We do not know each other, but I am so willing to be a subject for your book; I just thank you so much. What do you want me to do?

Well, greetings; this is where you get to tell your story and anything you wish to say about your whole death process.

Oh ok, readers, here I go. I'll regress just a bit. I was not in a very, we'll say, wealthy family—not even middle class. My father had left us. When I say *us*, it was me—I was the only son—and the rest were my sisters and my poor mother who was working as hard as she could. We couldn't make ends meet, really.

So the best thing I knew to do was that I joined this gang. We would rob and then sell the goods to make money. I would bring it home. I always spent it on my family. I gave shoes to my sisters because we were very cold up in New England. I bought a coat for my mother, and it was not a fancy fur coat, but just a good, heavy wool coat. I justified all of my stealing and all that so that I could help my family. (After my review, I was forgiven all that, but I am getting ahead of my story. As the readers know, they can assume I'm dead at this point; so be it, [*chuckles*]. I don't feel dead—that's the main thing.)

Anyway, so there I was in this gang. It followed me into high school. I made fairly good grades, enough to graduate from high school, but I had no intention, no burning desire to go any further. Again it was money that was the main concern—always the money; always to have ends meet; always to provide for my family. Little did I know that my way of life really was going to bring me to a swift end.

I take a sigh now, because this is really hard to repeat, for it was kind of messy. I got into a knife fight with this other gang member. He was not in our gang but in another (*opposing*) gang. We used to have… There were these two gangs who got together and taunted each other. We ended up wounding or killing one (*another*).

Sure enough, I had this knife that was against the law to carry, but we all had one. So I had this opened and ready to use. There was this one guy and he was taunting me. I was kind of large for my age—I was just 18 by this time. We were well matched, but what I ended up doing is I made the mistake of picking on one of the guys who also had a brother in that gang. They ganged up on me.

I was wielding my knife and doing quite well when the other one (*brother*) snuck up behind me, took me around the neck and just cut my—you call it the *carotid artery*, I found out. It was spurting blood like you wouldn't believe! I think everybody in the group was in a fountain of my blood. Needless to say, I did not last very long. I just slumped into his (*adversary's*) arms.

Of course, by this time, the sirens were blasting down the street and everyone was yelling, *cops; cops!* You can't imagine how fast those gangs can disappear when the cops are coming. There were all sorts of places we could run to. We ran into other people's apartments. We ran into alleys; we just disappeared like a scurry of ants. Or I'll say that is what I used to do, because I was no longer living in that gang.

I was laying on the pavement. I was dead by then. My blood had come spurting out because he had cut me so deeply. So there I was, laying on the pavement. I was still alive in some sense, for I was standing beside my body and thinking, *whoa, how can this be? Uh... here is my body and I am standing out of it.* I took my foot to try to jiggle it. Of course, that did not work. My foot went right through it. I thought, *oh God!* By this time the cops were there, and I am thinking to myself, *oh God, I gotta get out of here, 'cause they're going to catch me and throw the book at me.*

You can see that I was not thinking clearly. My body is dead and yet I am still worried about being caught by the cops and needing to escape. The next thing I knew—I don't know how to put it—as soon as I said, *I got to get out of here,* I did!

I was roaring through this tunnel like I was shot out of a cannon. The next thing I knew, I was through the tunnel, standing up, no longer bleeding, although there was blood all over me. There was this guy standing there (*with me*). I thought, *oh, crap, who is he?* That was the least I wanted to do—to run into another cop! You see, I still felt like Joe (*not real name*) laying on the pavement, and the cops are after me.

(*Tape runs out side A. Readers, imagine how freaked out I became to find that the second side B had no recording on it. I put in new batteries, checked the different buttons to be sure they were properly set—to no avail. I moaned for Sananda and asked if* Merchant-Man *could come back and do a repeat—just the second half.*)

All right, beloved. It's 9:00 AM on Monday the 16th. I see you are having some recording problems. We will bring back the last participant. He is more than willing to repeat his piece. So I will step aside and let him speak again and keep our fingers crossed. Thank you, Sananda.

It is 9:20 AM; let us hope I have it correct now.

Thank you so much for coming again. I need to check this tape recording one more time, please. (Pause.) Thank you so much for putting up with all of this. I got the first half of your story transcribed where you had just arrived in Heaven, but you did not know it. You were questioning the Angel, thinking he was a cop that was in pursuit of you. If you would please pick up your story again, and I do apologize for your having to say it all over again.

Actually, I am enjoying this immensely. It kind of brings back memories of the problems one can have on Earth, doesn't it? If you were in Heaven with me, we would have no problem at all. *That is true. Now please continue your story.* All right.

Here was this guy standing by me, and I was thinking he was a cop. You can see how that did not make any sense—how disoriented I was. I had just left this body that had bled to death, and here I was, God knows where, and I was worried that this cop has followed me.

He said to me, *dear soul, you have had a very traumatic experience; please follow me so I can take you to the Caring Center where you can be attended to.* So I was in such a disoriented state that I followed along. You know, down on Earth with our gang, going into alleys and other people's apartments and all of that, following this guy where he was going to take me to a place where they were going to take care of me sounded like the way to go—a good option. So I decided that I would go with him.

He led me to this large building, actually, and led me to this room. The room was very clean. Certainly a better room than I had ever seen in my life. It was not cluttered with a lot of junk—just a few pieces of furniture. Everything was so pleasing. I felt safe. He said, *your clothes are very bloody, so why don't you take them off and kick off your shoes, then crawl between the clean sheets.* He brought me a towel with warm water so that I could wash the blood off of my face and hands and feel better.

I did that and laid back down in bed, and before I knew it, I was sound asleep. The next thing I knew, I was awake again and this guy was still there. He said, *alright, do you feel more rested?* I said, *yes, actually I am feeling quite good.* I felt around on my throat and could not feel a huge scab there. I did not get that. I had seen all my blood spurt out so I thought, *well maybe they had given me a transfusion or something while I was sleeping.* Anyway, I didn't bring up all of that. He said, *if you will please follow me again.* Well, he had led me to a safe place the first time, so I thought it would be OK to follow him to see where he was taking me this next time.

He took me into another building. These buildings are *huge,* and I did not remember seeing buildings like this where I had been on Earth, but anyway, who was I to question at this point? I just again followed him.

You know, in a gang, we are used to following each other. So I thought, *Ok, here we go again,* and I followed him. He took me into this building that had all kinds of computers and movie screens and things like that. I sat down—he had pointed to where he wanted me to go—so I sat down. There was this huge screen—a screen like I had never seen before. We certainly didn't have any in our one room flat where I lived with my mother and sisters. This kind of intrigued me.

As I sat down, the movie started playing. It was playing my whole life! I thought, *well, this is weird. How did they get pictures of my whole life so soon? Who had taken these movies? Was it a spy who was running a camera on me? How in the heck did they do this?*

Again, I did not say it out loud. I sat there and became enthralled because as soon as I looked at a scene, I could feel that. As I looked at my mother, I could feel her exhaustion. I just wanted to hold her, and I felt so sad for her. She looked so worn out. My sisters looked kind of bedraggled, but I did notice they had on their new shoes and my mother had on her new coat, so at least they had something. They were not just total paupers.

Then I saw scenes where I was in high school. I was with the gangs—had hooked up with the gangs. As I looked at it now, I thought, *boy, that was really a rough bunch.* I noticed I could keep right up with them. I was feeling a little proud, for I had carried my load. I wasn't the weak link in that bunch.

However, as the movie progressed, I felt less proud and then I felt kind of, *oh my, what have I done here?* Even as we stole, I had a feeling this isn't right. I, in some ways, felt apologetic and sad for the store that we had robbed. Towards the end of the movie, there was the fight. I looked at all the ways I had fought. Again I thought I had done pretty well there. I saw the brother sneak up behind me and I was thinking, *oh, oh, look out.* Of course, I was just shouting at myself who paid no attention to my shouts. The next thing I knew, he had grabbed me behind the neck and he had slit my throat.

I thought, *holy s---.* Of course, I did not say that word out loud, because I knew it was not appropriate here. But I was thinking it—*holy ---.* (It starts with an "*s*.") Here I am bleeding to death, obviously. Blood was everywhere. The next thing I knew, all the cops were there.

There was this body lying on the ground—I guess that was me. But I am here, so I don't get that one.

So after I had pondered on all of this for a while, the screen went blank. The guy standing next to me said, *alright, dear soul, come with me.* I thought to myself, *why is he calling me a dear soul?* Then he turned to me and said, *because you are one.* I thought, *holy s, he can read my mind.* The guy just smiled. Then this time I said, *well, who in h are you?* He said, *I am your Guardian Angel.* I retorted, *oh, you gotta be kidding.* He said, *no, I am your Guardian Angel.* Being a smart aleck, I said, *well, you didn't do such a good job of it when you let the guy slit my throat!* He just smiled again.

That was kind of the end of that conversation. He said again to me, *alright sir, please come with me.* I am so used to… When you are in the cops' offices, jails and stuff, they say, *do this* and *do that* and you darn well better *do this* and *do that.* He said, *follow me.* It was not anything different from what I was used to, so I just followed him. Why not, you know?

Then he took me to another room. I don't know if it was a room in the same building or what. It was a large room; it was almost crowded. There were a lot of people in there—40 or 50. As I looked around, I saw a couple of the gang members I used to fight against. I thought, *oh gosh.* At the time they were my enemies, so I did not dare go up to them because I did not want them to pull their knives on me again. I found a seat and just sat down.

Everybody was talking at once. This other guy entered the room. He was a very nice looking man—very clean. He had on his robe. I have never seen Jesus, but I remember seeing those biblical movies, and they all had on these same kind of robes that didn't have much color in them. But this guy came in and his robe looked like it had some purple—lavender color in it. It was just nice and clean and comfortable looking.

So he came in, sat down, and started talking to us—asked what we thought of our review. There was kind of blank *duh* as a response. Then he asked, *do any of you know where you are?* Again there was this *duh* response. Then he said, *you are in Heaven!* The other guys and I said, *you can say that again; this is the cleanest place; nobody is fighting. It certainly does feel like Heaven.* The facilitator smiled and said, *no, really, you are in Heaven.* Again there was this silence. *You could have dropped a pin---* I guess is the saying.

He said… Then some guy yells, *do you mean if we are in Heaven, we are all dead?* Again there was this silence. We all waited with half a breath. He said, *dear souls, you do not remember all of the details, but you had a very dangerous and difficult experience on Earth which killed your bodies. You then came to Heaven and recognized the man who was with you. That was your Guardian Angel, and he took you to the Caring Center where your wounds were healed—you fell asleep and were healed. He then took you to the Reviewing room. You saw that lifetime, felt it, and now you are here in this room and we are discussing it.*

He said, *I suppose psychologists would call this* group process *because we are going to be talking about your experiences and belief systems. We will help you to see other ways to look at something. In our world, meaning Heaven, we call that* retraining. *Therefore, you will be retrained on various things.*

We just talked like that then. There's no Time as we are used to in Heaven, so we just talked. He went from person to person: *tell us your death experience.* When he kept saying that, it kind of really brought it home. This really was death. So we all talked about our death experiences. When each of us had told our story, he asked, *well, is anybody hungry?*

We all threw up our hands because when we were on Earth, we were all starving. We never had enough to eat. He told us that our Angels would take us to the Dining Hall and he said, *you will find that every food that you can imagine is there for you—everything except meat. We do not eat animals in Heaven. However, there are so many delicious choices that you won't miss the meats. And wait until you see those desserts! Your sweet tooth will be satisfied. This Dining Hall is open 24/7 so you can come any time, any time and as many times as you wish to eat your fill. We recognize that most of you had not had enough to eat in that lifetime.*

So with that, he stood up; we all stood up. Each of us had our Guardian Angel with us which we just now have noticed was there. We followed him, and he took us to the Dining Hall. That place is huge! Talk about your best restaurant on Earth, this one had everything.

We kind of got in line but noticed you really did not need to do that. You could just go to the dessert area (they call them *stations*) or to the salad bar or to where the soup was. You did not have to stay in line. It seemed as if everything flowed. You took a tray that was there and took your bowl of soup to a table, sat down and ate the soup. Then you could just leave the used dish there while you went and got something else and brought that back. When you went back to your table with that, your dirty bowl and tray had disappeared. You had a whole new set of utensils.

We ate our fill, chatted with whoever had sat down near us. I noticed the two gang members who had kind of recognized me. So I thought what the h and walked over to them. I said, *well, I see you two did not make it either!* They looked a little sheepish and replied, *nope; nope, I got it in the gut and he got it in the face.*

I said, *well gosh, you wouldn't know it. There are no scars on your face.* He said, *yes, that's what's great about this place. They ought to have this down on Earth.* So anyway, we chatted a little bit and ate more food together. Then our Angels said, *now where does everyone want to bed down for the night?* They used our way of talking because that was the way we were used to thinking. We did not realize that anything you thought would manifest.

The Angels took us to what looked like a large dormitory. We each had a nice clean room and a clean bed. Everyone said, *well, where is the bathroom for a shower?* We were showed the communal showers. There were no toilets, but no one noticed that because we did not have to go to the toilet, which seems kind of odd, as I think about it.

We showered and there was a clean robe to put on. Most of us were in green robes, for we know now that was a healing color. But some on them had on blue, too, for that would bring them peace. They needed peace from their experience. So we had our robes on and sort of just pitter pattered back to our rooms in the dormitory. It was just like in the Army, except we had separate cubicles for our beds. Everyone had a nice bed, a sink, and a chair. We just went in and called that *home.* For some of us, that was home, for it was better than what we had had on Earth.

We all went to our beds and did not think that much about it. But as soon as we laid down on our bed, we were out like a light! We just slept. We did not know we were still being healed during those times.

I am trying to think of what else… In the morning when we woke up, of course, there was a lot of chitter-chatter going on. Since we had had showers the night before, we did not do much in the morning. Some guys shaved; others didn't bother. Everybody wanted to go to breakfast. We weren't about to miss a meal, you understand.

Groups of us went to the Dining Hall and loaded up on—oh gosh— loaded up on pancakes. And there were waffles; some wanted French toast and sausages. Oh, no, there were no sausages, per se, but sausages made from vegetables. They looked like sausages, but they weren't meat. They were very tasty; you couldn't tell the difference, so why not? We ate that, filled up on the waffles and pancakes, smeared on the butter and poured on the maple syrup. It was wonderful!

Then after we ate breakfast, we met again in our group room. The facilitator was there. He talked more about our belief systems. We got used to the fact it was our retraining room, and we would meet there every day for a long period, for we needed much retraining.

Now let's see what else… I think that is it—all I can think of. You had some questions last time, but you will have to remind me. *Yes, and you will have to remind me! When I am channeling like that, I don't remember what I have said afterwards. So I will look through my notes and see if I can come up with those questions plus some new ones.*

Questions (Q) and Answers (A)

Q: How old were you when you died?

A: *I was 18 when I graduated high school; I think 20 or 21, when I died.*

Q: And how long has it been since you have had a body?

A: *That I don't know; I have the same body that I did on Earth. I can't give you a time on that. As I have said, Heaven does not have Time (as known on Earth);*

Q: What was your purpose in that lifetime?

A: *Hmm, that's a good one. I guess it was to provide for my sisters and my mother. I provided the best way that I could. I provided without violence. Even though we stole these things; there was no violence. We did not kill in order to get someone's money. At least I didn't. I stole a car or I stole something else. If you could steal a car, that would give you the most money. That would give me enough money so I could buy Mom the warm coat, my sisters their shoes and stuff.*

Q: Did you talk about reincarnation in your group?

A: *Oh yes, a lot of the guys want to go back and have everything they did not have before—big houses and fancy cars. But I am not interested in that. I just want to be comfortable.*

Q: What will you have as your new vocation?

A: *Actually, I want to help children. Since I helped my sisters, you see, I would like to do something to help the children. I am good with my hands—maybe build equipment for parks—anything that would help the children. I know I will need more education—maybe a couple of years in college, just to learn, you know, the professional way to help the kids.*

Q: What was your biggest regret?

A: *My biggest regret was in joining those—I am not swearing anymore so I will say—darn gangs. That just led me down the tubes. That was not a good choice. I had some other choices. I could have gotten a job—something that would support me, my mother and sisters. But I didn't. I just joined a gang. I seemed to like that violence. I have a regret about that. And yes, I am being retrained. Violence is not the answer.*

Q: Have you met any of your past relatives—any of them who had gone on ahead of you?

A: *There were people coming up to me saying they were Uncle so-and-so or Aunt so-and-so. I did not know who they were, so I was just polite with them, but I didn't feel like striking up a relationship of any kind.*

Q: I want to ask you… I have yet to hear anyone talk about their pets. Did you have a pet and have you seen any pets that others may have in Heaven?

A: *Well, you know when you were as poor as we were, you did not spend money on dog food and things like that. So I can't say I had a pet. I know there is a special section where people's animals are. They can meet them there. Some people who have evolved and have their own house or apartment have reunited with their animal. I know that happens. But I am not the best one to talk to about that because I don't know anything about it.*

Q: Did you discuss any religions?

A: *Oh boy, did we! Our group was mostly Catholic, and we were told by the facilitator that all the religions were made by men, which I don't quite understand. They said those religions had scribes—you know the ones who write down the stories—who would make up the stories to match the way they felt. In that way, man made the religions.*

The Catholic religion was very heavy into that—a lot of sin and all of that. Our facilitator told us that most of that is not true (sin). So there is a lot of retraining with all of that.

Q: Do you have a job that you go to that has a title? On Earth you could be a school teacher or a baker, something like that.

A: *Oh no, not yet. There are a lot of volunteer jobs. If you want to do something, you can volunteer. I like working in the shoe shop. You know, I gave shoes to my sisters, so I am learning how to make shoes. I enjoy doing that, but I don't go every day. Another time I like to go to the bakery and punch down the bread. I enjoy that—stuff of that nature.*

Q: Are you finding you still like to have food or are you getting to the point where you will not be drawn to eat three times a day?

A: *Yeah, actually I have passed that. I go now just to socialize, so to speak—see the guys. But lots of time I am involved in punching down the bread or making some shoes; I forget to go eat. So I guess I am gradually getting away from that.*

Q: All right, I thank you for your flexibility in coming again—telling me your story AGAIN. I do apologize for that; the recorder acted up on me. Is there any question you would still like to ask me? I can't remember what we even discussed last time.

A: *No, you answered it already, so I do not need to repeat it. I thank you for remembering me and having me back. I thoroughly enjoyed it, actually. So I will say any time you want to chat away, just call me* (chuckles).

Alright, thank you so much and God bless you in any of your endeavors for your next life time.

Thank you so much!

You are quite welcome. This interview is finished at last. Bye for now.

Goodbye.

Whew, Sananda, I think I am done. After I check to see that the recording was successful, I will be delighted.

I think all is well, dear one, but you may want to order another recorder just to have it on hand. Yes, by all means (I bought my new Sony through Amazon). Thank you, Sananda. *You are welcome, my love; over and out.*

8 CHIEF-MAN

O3-18-15 *Alright, dear one, let's give this another go, shall we? (10:10 AM) This next Being had a troubled life, as you will soon find out, but for us who are writing a book, a very interesting one. I will step aside now and let him say his piece.*

Hello, dear Author of the book you are writing. I am the next in line for giving you my experience. I am told my code name will be *Chief-Man* which I think is rather interesting in that I was a Chief so to speak to the group of people I had around me.

I was a gang member also and I was able to give my crew orders left and right. I was not from a privileged home. I had little education, but I was fiercely competitive. I wanted to excel in everything I did. For that time and where I was, that is exactly what I did. I exceled in everything.

I put together a gang that was feared throughout cities. Everyone knew my reputation. My family had more or less evicted me—gave up on me. I was considered the bad seed of the family, simply because I would not allow my father to dictate to me what I was going to do, where it was going to be, what I had to wear. You cannot imagine what it was like to be continuously harassed in your own family.

My mother was what you would call a *milk-toast,* so to speak. How she ended up marrying this bully, I have no idea. I had very little respect for everyone in my family.

Therefore, I went out on my own. I did not even finish high school. I saw no gain in it for me. It was like, *what was it doing for me?* Nothing that I could see. I was better than the kids who were there. Even though my education was not very high, I could think better. I talked back to the teachers, which they did not like. That put me in the Principal's office many times. My punishment was to stay after school, and it was all just a bunch of crap.

I was so relieved when they just basically kicked me out of school. You see, that was my excuse, as I was roaming the streets and bringing people to me. The cops would say, *aren't you supposed to be in school?* I'd say, *no, I was kicked out.* So what were they going to do with that? I could not go back to school because the school wouldn't have me! Since it was such a tough neighborhood, the cops just kind of shrugged their shoulders and really didn't want to get too close to me, for they knew we could be quite vicious.

Life kind of progressed on that level, and I was in many fights. I was the *kingpin,* and I did not tolerate anyone going against my word. I guess it was much from my father, since he would not allow anyone else but him to speak in that house. I more or less copied him. Now *I* was, you could say, the bully of my group. It is interesting that many of those lads needed that. They wanted somebody to power over them. And boy, could I do that. I loved it.

Well, needless to say, that was not going to go on very long, was it, before I ended up in the hospital or dead or something else. As fate would have it, I ended up dead. I was shot. What can one say? There was a fight and we all pulled out our guns and blasted away at each other. We didn't even have to take aim because there were so many of us, someone would be bound to get hit. Little did I think I would be the one hit! I guess now that is known as bad karma. So that was the end of my Earth life—short but not all that sweet. I was only 17 or 18 when I got it.

As I look back on my life, that was barely a beginning. When you think now people can live up into their seventies, in some ways it was a waste. However, I did not know any different *then*. I had to learn all of that after I got up here.

Now you readers might be thinking, *well, it doesn't sound as if he was a very good—what would be the right word—candidate for Heaven.* You would expect me to go straight to Hell. I kind of agree with you. But you see, it happened so fast—I was shot in the forehead where you are out like a light. The next thing I knew I was standing up again, and there is this guy with me who I had never seen before. He seemed to be on my side (*empathic*).

I said, *what are you doing here?* He said, *well actually, I came to look after you, sir.* I liked that he called me *sir.* That meant I was again with someone who appreciated my authority and he was saying *sir.* Anyway, he said, *come along, sir. I need to take you to the Caring Center so that your wounds can be healed.* I am thinking to myself, *wounds (?) What other wounds did I have! I was shot in the head and that was that.* But apparently I had other gunshot wounds and hadn't even noticed them. It was like I did not have time to notice them; the shots came so rapidly with everyone shooting. Now I am finding I was shot in the arm; in the leg. Good gosh! I could have been a pin cushion if I had stayed alive, but I hadn't. I drew the wrong card and was whisked away.

I found out later that I had made it to Heaven and I thought to myself, *Jesus, I don't know how that happened.* I was not the purest of the pure to land in Heaven. I went to church once in a while; I was Catholic. All that gang were Catholics. Seems like the poor people were always Catholic.

We were always being told what to do, what to think by the Pope who was talking to the Priests who were talking to the Nuns. Boy, you were getting a big dose of religion whether you wanted it or not. It did not necessarily mean we needed it. You were just brow-beaten by this religion and all of it says *you have sinned; you have done this and done that. You aren't going to go to Heaven if you keep this up.*

They put such a fear package into the kids that whether we believed the religion or not, we believed that the Pope-the Priests-the Nuns were telling us we were sinners. We took on that stigma—*we are sinners*. Isn't that an interesting thought?

So I am carrying this stigma with me up to where I am finding out is Heaven, and this guy who said he is my Angel is calling me *sir*. So now I really am confused, because I am thinking, *well, does that mean that when you are a sinner, you are also in some way addressed as sir, with respect?* According to the Pope-the Priests-the Nuns down there (*Earth*), I would not have a prayer (*of reaching Heaven*). These are all just thoughts I have kept in my head.

I followed this guy who claimed he was an Angel, simply because I had no place else to go. Everything was so new to me. I thought *OK, why not? If he is taking me to Hell or if he is taking me to Heaven, I'll soon find out.*

He takes me to this building—this *huge* building—if you were home on Earth, you would definitely be in a five star hotel or something like that. So he takes me to this building with flowers all on the outside. I am thinking to myself, *what kind of building is this? Is this a hospital?*

I have never seen a hospital that had all of these gardens and stuff before. Anyway, I found out later this guy, this Angel, could hear everything I said (*thought*). If I had known that, I would have kept my tongue a little cleaner. Anyway, so be it.

He took me to this room. I realize now that this building was called the *Caring Center*—sort of like what we would think of as a hospital on Earth, except it was not set up like a hospital. You did not see people running around in white coats and stethoscopes hanging around their neck or anything like that.

We just went into this room. Nobody examined me or anything as I was thinking, *gosh, I must really be in bad shape.* I couldn't figure how I had gotten there because this bullet had gone through my head. I thought, *well, maybe in some way, it had missed vital parts. You always hear of those kinds of miracles you know.*

Anyway, the guy told me to take off my clothes; they were all splattered with blood and had holes in them from the bullets. I took them off; kicked my shoes off and sat on the bed. He brought me a towel with some warm water on it and said, *now wash your face and your hands so you will feel a little cleaner; then climb into bed.* I did this and I must say I didn't realize how tired I was; I just fell into bed and I took a few deep breaths and the next thing I knew, I went to sleep—just went to sleep.

During that time—I used to dream a lot when I was a kid, so—I was at somebody's funeral. I don't know who it was (*for*). There was everybody I knew. My parents were there. My father was looking very stoic and righteous. My mother was looking very pathetic per usual. They seemed to be kind of murmuring. I couldn't hear what they were saying. I didn't stay very long. Funerals were not my thing on Earth, so anyway.

I slept and the next thing I knew I woke up. This guy was still there. He said, *are you feeling better?* I said, *yeah, I am feeling less tired, if that is what you mean.* He asked, *do you hurt any place?* I wiggled around and was surprised because if you have a gunshot go through your leg or your arm, it is going to feel sore, man, because I had those before. But I had never had one in the head. I wiggled around and said, *no, I feel fine;* I tried to find those bullet holes and could not find any. *Where are those holes?* He said, *they were healed while you were sleeping.* I said, *wow, this is some hospital to be able to heal you that fast!*

He said *alright, now we are going into another area.* At this time I noticed I had on a clean robe. That kind of peaked my curiosity; it was a green robe. So I asked how I had got this on. He said, *the Angels put this on you while you were sleeping.* I thought, *that was a good trick, but here I am with a robe on, so they must have done that.*

Again I followed him and we went into another building. This building was just as enormous as the last one I was in. The gardens were all immaculate. I thought, *boy, this must have cost someone a pretty penny.*

He took me into the building. There were all these computers and huge movie screens. People were looking at the screens—some were crying and others were just sitting there stunned. I was thinking, *boy, I hope they don't show me those movies! I like Westerns, myself.* Anyway, he showed me where to sit.

I no sooner sat down when my screen started lighting up. There I was looking at my life. I thought to myself, *oh, what a mess that was. I am just better out of that. That lifetime was awful. I don't want to ever repeat that.* Of course, the movie started way back when I was a baby and ended with the gun fight. I saw how nasty my father was and how I reacted to his authority and his being a bully. And my mother, how pathetic she was. She never stood up for me. God, what a crummy family I was in. I was lucky I left when I did. I can't think much more to say about, that so I just stood up and said to the guy, *I'm through here. This movie bores me.*

He said, *sit down, sir, there is just a speck more to see.* I thought that was funny; he wasn't going to let me leave until the whole thing had finished and the credits came on. I sat down and thought, *oh, what the h or hell.* Instead of looking, I just closed my eyes; *enough of this crap; I'm not going to watch this.* So I closed my eyes, but the amazing thing was the movie kept playing in my head. Even with my eyes closed I saw everything and felt everything. I thought, *good lord, this is ridiculous!*

Anyway, I sat through the whole thing and felt it all and thought, *oh God, this is a crappy movie; I'm glad I do not have to watch it anymore.* Then the movie just turned off and my eyes that were still shut just went blank. I opened them and the screen now was blank. So I stood up and said, *OK, can I go now? Yes,* he said, *we are finished here. But you will need to follow me, for I need to take you to one more place.*

I thought to myself, *now what?* But by this time... You know you get to the point when you just kind of... You'll go along like a sheep just because you are fed up with it all. It's like, *crime-an-ee, there's no place else to go, I might as well.*

He took me into this room. There were all kinds of people in there. Some were derelicts, so to speak. Some were white trash. I thought, *God, what a bunch of losers!* I did not want to say it out loud, because I did not know where I was yet. We were told by the guys to take a seat. We sat down and the chairs were quite comfortable, which surprised me.

This man came in who was called the *facilitator* and he greeted us very nicely—very warmly and said, *now, my dear souls...* They talked like that which I always thought was like religion and wanted to gag, but anyway… He says, *my dear souls*—we all stared at him—he said, *now, do you all know where you are? Is there anyone who does not know where he is?* Of course, a lot of hands shot up. He said, *well, I will just fill you in. You have just had your experience on Earth. During that time, whether you realize it or not, you died.* Then there was a chorus of *died?* He said, *yes, you died. So where do you think you are now?*

I said, *well, we were told by the Pope-the Priests-the Nuns that we were all sinners, so I guess since I am a sinner, this could be Hell but it is a pretty plush Hell.* He said, *is there anyone else with some ideas?* Some people agreed with me while others did not.

The facilitator said, *actually, you are in Heaven—you made it into Heaven!* I said, *I'll be God-damned. We made it into Heaven! We are not as much of a sinner as the Pope-the Priest-the Nuns said (we were).* Anyway, we questioned him and he told us different things, saying we were in Heaven.

So that is about all I can tell you. I know when this guy, this Being who had a lot of Light, came to me and asked if I would tell my story and I said I would, he went on and said there would be a period of questions and answers. So I guess at this point I will just shut up and let you ask the questions.

Alright, thank you for your story; it was very interesting. And yes, I do have some questions. Many of the questions I have asked the others. I will repeat them to you, for they will be new to you.

Questions (Q) and Answers (A)

Q: You have already said how old you were when you died (17-18). Can you tell me what your purpose was in that lifetime?

A: *Jesus, I never thought of it as having a purpose. I was just there doing my thing. I did not know it had a purpose. No, I don't know what my purpose was.*

Q: Did you finish your contract?

A: *I don't know what you mean by that. I did not know we had a contract for this (life). I don't remember signing anything; I don't quite know where you are coming from.*

Q: What was your biggest regret?

A: *My biggest regret was I did not rise higher in my circle. I got just so far and then stuck there. I regretted also all the religion of the Pope-the Priests-the Nuns (said in staccato), if that is a regret.*

Q: Are you being what is known as retrained?

A: *Well, that facilitator in that group room said we would be meeting there every day and that was all part of retraining our beliefs and what we had been up to. So you could say we were being retrained, but I am not quite sure what about, unless it had to do with the Pope-the Priests-the Nuns who all said we were sinners. But he (facilitator) is saying in the retraining that there was no sin; we did not sin. So we are just learning about that; we're still confused about that.*

Q: Have you met any of your past relatives?

A: *Hmm, I've met some, but I don't really know who they were.*

Q: What about pets—did you have any pets that had already died before you and you have seen again?

A: *No, I wasn't into pets all that much. They cost a lot of money, and I did not want to spend money on food and stuff like that.*

Q: Have you done any traveling since you have been in Heaven?

A: *I know there are places to go, but I haven't the hang of this place yet. I am a little leery of straying too far away because I am afraid I would not be able to find my way back.*

Q: Do you have a job in Heaven that would have a title for it like a baker or something of that nature?

A: *Well, me and the guys are still learning the ropes, (so no).*

Q: How long has it been since you died?

A: *It wasn't all that long ago. I can't remember exactly. I remember it was around when President Kennedy got shot—so whenever that was (Nov. 22, 1963). It hasn't been very long (ago).*

Q: How about watching events on Earth. Do you do that?

A: *Yeah, there is a group of us who like to go do that. The problem is... We like to watch the fights, but they don't show any of those. They have ballet, and I am not about to watch that. They have opera, and I am not about to watch that. They have swimming matches. I like that. You always want your favorite to win and stuff like that.*

Q: Tell me about your living quarters.

A: *That was a surprise because the group that I met where we get retrained were all taken to this building. We were told that we could take one of the rooms and sleep there and live there. Or if we wanted to we could build our own house if we lived there (in Heaven) long enough. I am thinking,* holy cow, that would take too much work. I am not about to do that, *so I just took what was provided. They had very nice comfortable rooms— sort of like a dormitory. So some other guys and I live there.*

Q: Do you still eat food?

A: *I am not about to give up my favorite foods, so yeah, we go to the Dining Hall and eat—whenever we want to actually.*

Q: We are coming to the end of our interview. Is there anything you would like to ask me?

A: *I am not quite sure how I am able to talk to you, but I think you can hear me.*

Yes, I am hearing you very well.

And you are going to put everything that I have said into a book?

Yes. I am writing this book on the different ways people died and their experiences in Heaven. Here on Earth not everyone has that information about Heaven.

Oh, I see; it is a Manual on Heaven, huh?

Yes, I guess you could put it that way. It is a good way to think about it.

Well I wish you luck; that's a hard one. I did not read that much when I had my Earth life. If I were still there, I think that would be fun.

Q: Do you plan to reincarnate one of these days?

A: *Oh yeah, I suppose. When you lived a life like I did, I understand you have to go back and repeat it and try to do it a different way. But I just hope I do not have to have the same parents, because he sure was a bully.*

Q: Do you have any other things you would like to say to me?

A: *No, to thank you, I guess. I've enjoyed this. This has been interesting.*

Q: I am glad. I have enjoyed it also, and I wish you all the luck in your next endeavor. May God bless you. Bye for now…

Bye.

(10:50 AM)

9 CLERGY-MAN

03-22-15 Good morning, my precious one; you are all ready to bring in the 9th chapter. Yes, I am; thank you Lord. Alright, we'll just get right at it then. I'll step aside and he will speak. Thank you Lord.

Hello to you; I don't know what I am supposed to do, but I am here. Thank you for bringing me here, I guess.

Hello back to you; I am the author of this book. You will be given the code name of Clergy-Man. Were you a clergy in your last lifetime by any chance?

No, that was not my gig, shall we say.

Alright then, just tell me and the readers... Everything you say will be put in the book. Be as descriptive as you possibly can be.

OK. Well, I was born into a poor family in a small town in the Midwest. (I've been cautioned not to say names of things.) It was a typical time of growing up. The farmers were struggling—not quite the *dust bowl*, but it was getting that way.

My father worked from dawn to dusk and my mother kept right up with him in the kitchen, always canning anything she could get her hands on. The winters were very cruel, and they relied heavily on what she had canned during the (*produce*) season. She was not the only one.

Our neighbors were all doing the same thing. But we did the best we could, and since everybody was in the same boat, so to speak, there were periods of laughter. We got together and had our potluck lunches or suppers. We had dancing in the barn. The moving pictures depict that life quite well, actually.

So I was probably around 5-6 or something like that. It was winter time. I developed what was called the *croup*. The little kids were coughing and coughing. The mothers had their tea kettles boiling on the stove to bring some humidity to the air to see if that would help the children to cough up the junk.

Anyway, I had it real bad and I coughed and coughed. Before I knew it, I had coughed myself right out of my body! Now I know that for people who are reading this book, it may seem incredulous, but it happened to more of the children than one realized in the pioneer days.

Of course, my parents grieved but also it left one less mouth to feed. I was not the only boy in the family. I had brothers and sisters. The parents had little else to do in the winter but to snuggle and love and bring forth another baby. So all the families were quite large and most of the families had had babies and older who had died of various ailments.

So here I am outside my body. Although I was only around 6 years old, as soon as I was outside of my body, I felt older. I didn't feel six. In fact, there was a part of me that knew more than the part that had been in my body. Of course, I was able to view the whole family getting hysterical, and my poor mother was trying her very best to bring some life back to me. In those days they put mustard plasters on your chest and so she put a new one on me in hoping I would come back to life. They were not sure if I was dead, but they did their best.

As I stood outside of my body, I not only found out I knew more than I used to know while in the body, but I had a new friend with me. We immediately struck it off and were what you say, *buddies.* I said to him, *what is happening here? What's going on?* He said, *oh, you will get used to it. You know, you just vacated your body. It's not such a big deal. Come; I'll show you the ropes.* I said, *what about my mother and father and stuff? What do I do about them?* He said, *just say goodbye to them or something like that. Or thanks, I'm on my way; say anything you want to say.* So I just kind of yelled to them, *Ok, Mom, Dad, sisters and brothers, hmm, thanks for everything, but I'm off. I'll see you later, I guess.*

I said to the boy (*who was with me*), *Ok, now what do I do?* He said, *just follow me.* He took me to what looked like an entrance to a tunnel and said, *don't be surprised because you are really going to whoosh through this.* I said, *what is this?* He said, *it is a tunnel.* I said, *Ok.* Sure enough, as I came closer to it, I could feel a suction; it just sucked me and WHOOSH away I went. He had taken hold of my hand and we held hands all the way through the tunnel. When we got to the end there was a bright light and lush greenery. I said, *wow!* Now I was not speaking like a little 6 year old; I seemed to be more adult. I said, *gosh, what is this place?* He turned to me and said, *congratulations, you made it to Heaven.* I exclaimed, *Heaven (!); wait until I tell Mom. And wait until I tell Dad. They were always talking to their neighbors and everyone else saying that so and so wasn't going to go to Heaven. Then here **I** am.* At the same time, what was kind of strange was this person I was with had grown! He was no longer a boy like me. He was a man. I said, *gosh, what happened to you? Are you the same guy?* He said, *yes, I am your Guardian Angel, and I can change all shapes whenever I wish.* By this time, I am talking like an older person myself, so I said, *Ok, I guess I have to believe that since I saw it all happen, but it sure doesn't seem very real.* He said, *it's real. Now, come with me because I need to take you to the Care Center so that they can heal that croup that you had.* I said, *yeah, I have never coughed so hard in my life. I felt strangled.* He said, *you* *will soon feel wonderful.* I asked, *is it like a hospital?* He said, *you can say that, but it is a lot more caring and much more personal.*

He brought me to this huge building, and we went inside. He took me to this very nice room. It was so shiny and all painted in yellow which made the room look so bright and clean. As I looked, there wasn't any dust on the window or window sill. Everything was so shiny and clean.

He said, *alright young sir.* He started calling me *sir* which I thought was strange. Anyway, *young sir, take off your clothes now for they are very dusty and your shoes. I will get you a cloth with warm water so you can wash the dust off your face and hands. Then climb in between the sheets and take a nice nap.* I said, *well, since I just got out of bed, I don't feel like a nap.* He said, *come, take your clothes off.* He said it in a very loving but a commanding voice. I knew then that I needed to do it. So I climbed into bed after washing my face and hands. The bed was so comfortable and smelled good. It had a wonderful clean scent to it. As soon as I laid down on the pillow, I felt sleepy. I closed my eyes, and before I knew it, I was out—just sound asleep.

Then I had this dream where I was at my own funeral. I thought, *well, this is strange,* but I saw my parents. It was a particular funeral for those days. Everything looked kind of tattered and dusty and forlorn. But they did the best they could. They had gathered some flowers out of someone's yard. There was my body laid out. Everybody was crying—even my brothers and sisters, which kind of shocked me.

But then as I poked people and yelled at them, nobody could see or hear me. I said to this Angel who has been by my side now and was still there—he even came with me in my dreams—*you know, I don't want to stay around here. I can't talk to anybody and nobody sees me. I've seen enough, so I just want to go back to Heaven.* That was the end of that dream.

I remembered hearing soothing music, and the next thing I knew I was awake again. I was standing up and my friend was still there. He said, *alright, young sir, how are you feeling now? Oh, much better; I'm not even coughing.* He said, *no, that was healed while you were sleeping.* I said, *they must have given me a bath because look, I have this green robe on.* He said, *the Angels cleaned you up a bit while they healed you. They did not want to put your dusty clothes back on you, so you are wearing a robe that most of the people wear.* I noticed he too had a robe on now. It was a white, actually. He said, *alright young sir, we've got to go to another building. Oh, is this where I could go and have some breakfast?* He said, *are you hungry?* I thought about it and replied, *well, not particularly, but I always had breakfast when I got up in the morning.* He said, *well, all of that will be taken care of in a little while.*

He took me to this other building. I have never seen buildings that big before. I was amazed because where I lived (*on Earth*), the buildings were just small, made of boards, had tin roofs, one floor—maybe just two rooms. And here is this huge building. He took me to this room with all of these movies going on, I guess. He said, *you will have your own movie all by yourself over there. Go take a seat.* He pointed in the direction, and I went over there and sat down in front of this large screen.

I noticed my body is no longer the 6 year old. I have a body like a teen ager. All of this was confusing to me. I felt the same but my body was different. So I had all of these questions going through my mind.

I sat in front of the screen and he told me I would have my own personal movie. *No one in this room has a movie like you are going to see.* Of course you have all of these questions going around in your head. I, of course, told him, *I am confused at this point. I don't know what is going on.* Then I thought it would be better to just shut up and watch. I never was one for talking that much, so I just obediently sat down and turned my attention to the screen.

The movie had already started. There I was as a baby with my family. I noticed how everything compared to this building I was in now was kind of shabby and poor. Gosh, all the dust was everywhere. My father was in his overalls and my mother had on her apron. There were all the kids. We had a cow so at least we had milk. My mother was able to make bread. We had cheese from the milk too. We had hens so we had eggs. So we ate a fairly good breakfast.

I was watching all of that and *feeling* the impatience of the kids, but feeling the hopelessness from my father. That surprised me! Because, as you know, as a kid growing up, you do not realize that to your father and mother, things were not as rosy as you were led to believe. As I watched and I could feel it, we really were poor. My father was doing the best he could to provide for us. My mother just looked worn out—having all those kids and having the canning she had to do.

So I watched all of that. Needless to say, my movie was not as long as some other people's I noticed in the room. They were sitting there when I arrived, and they were still sitting there watching their movie when I left. Later on I said to my Angel, *why are some people's movies longer than mine was?* He said, *because they lived longer. You only lived for six years. Your movie was short. Some of these people lived into their nineties, so they are sitting there for a long time. They are experiencing all that they had lived through.*

He said, *your family while you were poor did love you and you felt that.* I said, *yes I felt loved; I didn't feel where they or somebody was being mean to me. We kids fought, but I did not feel any real meanness about it all.* Anyway, we chatted a little bit and then he told me we were going to another room. I question, *another one? Is this another movie?* He said, *no, you will be meeting with a group of people who were pretty much where you are.* I said, *I am not understanding that.*

You know that you have a soul for your body. I said, *well, I learned that in church, but I do not know what it means.* He said, *it is that energy of you, from your Higher Self. It comes into your body. Souls grow, just like when you went to school and you went from one grade to another. We call that evolution. Well, your soul is evolving, so the room we are going to has souls who are at about the same stage as you are. It is like in school. Some of your brothers and sisters are in high school. Some are in grade school. When you were on Earth, you were just getting through kindergarten. So the souls are at different stages.*

However, in Heaven you are joining a group where the souls are quite evolved—you know, more advanced. You could say if they were in school, they would be going into college. Of course, I was just kind of overwhelmed with it then and not quite understanding it all. I just kind of looked at him, and he could tell I was not understanding what he was saying.

He brought me into this room. Here were all of these other people. He kind of whispered to me, *you see, all of these people are at the stage that your soul is at. This is the stage your soul was at when you died.* Of course, I did not get it. Here I was only 6 and my soul was already in college! Anyway…

The room was crowded. I was thinking, *there are sure a lot of kids here.* He said, *actually there are. Most everyone in this room died around the same age as you did. They had different deaths, but they were all around 6 years old also.* I said, *Ok, 6 years old going to college.* He said, *you got it!* Well, I hadn't got it yet, but it was sinking in a little more clearly.

Since we were all kids, I'll put it that way, and since we all knew we had died, he said, *Ok and how did you die, and how did you die? Well, I had the croup and I couldn't breathe. And how did you die? Well, I fell down the well. And how did you die? Well, I went out in a snow storm and could not find my way back and got frozen. And how did you die?* It went on and on and on. It was quite amazing. I had not realized that so many people had died the same time that I had died. Then my Angel, who could read my thoughts, said, *well, the world is a very large place. So there are hundreds and thousands of people who died at the age of six.* I said, *oh Ok, and they all went to Heaven.* He said, *some did and some didn't.* I pondered on that a while.

The *facilitator* for the room came in—that's what they called him. I would have called him a *teacher.* He had these—I don't know how to explain it—Lights that came out of him. My Angel whispered to me, *that's called an aura.* I said, *oh, but why is he shining like a Christmas tree and we are all like Christmas trees without lights?* He said, *look again.* I could see, if you called us a tree, we had a light shining here and there. But we weren't flooded like the teacher was. So he talked to us. I don't know how long we were there. He mainly was telling us things that most of us did not quite understand. Then he said, *alright that is enough for today. We will meet here tomorrow.*

By this time, most of us were tired from our tunnel trip, we'll call it. But we found out later that not everyone went through the tunnel. That got me confused again, and I turned to my Angel and he was reading my mind and said, *you'll understand all of that eventually. Just let it go for now. I'm taking you to breakfast now. Breakfast!* That's wonderful. He said, *I will take you to the Dining Hall.*

When we got there, I was astounded, while the other kids who were from a more affluent family or a more prosperous family were not that surprised. But for me, seeing that abundance was like being in a dream. I might wake up and be back in a dusty room eating some chicken eggs.

But this food that was laid out on the tables… The fresh fruit I had never seen before, all the different breads and muffins and biscuits with gravy, eggs in any way you could even conceive of. So I piled my plate high and took it to a table where other guys were stuffing themselves. Some went back for more. I had taken so much the first time that I could not eat any more.

My Angel was still there and he told me he would be taking me to where I would be sleeping and I could call that my *little bit of Heaven.* He took me to what would be a dormitory. Sure enough, there were a bunch of guys from our group there also. It was the nicest surprise I could imagine—to think I had my own room. I couldn't believe it. *I have my own room with a comfortable bed; everything is so clean. There's my sink and look how shiny it is.* I turned the faucet on and all this clean water came out. There wasn't any dirt any place. There was a clean robe hanging in a small closet. I couldn't believe it. As soon as I thought of something, it would appear. I went to the sink and thought, *I have not brought a tooth brush,* and I opened a small cabinet over the sink and there was a tooth brush. I needed some tooth paste and there was the toothpaste. I didn't have a comb and brush, and they appeared. It went on like that. I was kind of amazed with it all.

I went out of my little room and everyone was talking at once about what happened to him. We couldn't believe the luxuries that we had now compared to home.

I was told you might have some questions for me. I can't think of anything else I could say, but when you ask me questions, it will bring up ideas for me.

Thank you so much; it was a very interesting story. And yes, I do have questions for you.

Questions (Q) and Answers (A)

Q: In your group discussion, did the facilitator discuss anything about your pre-life contracts?

A: *Yeah, he did. He said that as we each take a life, we have that life pretty well set up for us—who will be our parents, who will be our brothers and sisters; how long that life will be. There was a contract. He said that some of you will see you are meant to die early, and there are reasons for that. Others will live for a long time; there are reasons for that. You understand everything that is set up for you, but at the same time there is free will so that there can be changes in that contract. There are what we call* windows of opportunity *so that there are several windows where you can decide to die or not to die. Now take that example of you who died of the croup. You took that window and died because that was your contract, but you could have waited and in some way not died— maybe you were able to cough up that phlegm that choked you so that you did not die of that. But you would have died several years after that because that would be your next window. Do you understand? By this time we were grasping it a little bit better, so yes, we did discuss contracts.*

Q: Did you have a beloved pet of some kind who had died before you?

A: *Well, living on the farm, we did have pets. I had a pet pig and, of course, we kids always had a lamb or calf or something like that. But I have not seen any of them since I have been here.*

Q: Are you still eating and drinking or have you given that up?

A: *I more or less have given that up for now. I can still go to the Dining Hall when I want to, but I find that I get involved with other things, and I am not really thinking about food any more.*

Q: What are your activities? Are you doing different things now? You sort of left the readers where you had a wonderful dormitory room. Have you been doing anything else?

A: *Well, there is a huge Library here, so I go there because it has lots of books I have never seen before. I find that I am interested in that. I don't know how I did it but I am able to read them, so I am reading some of the books.*

Q: Have you traveled any since you have been in Heaven?

A: *You know, there was a group of us that were not able to travel in that lifetime—remember we were all around the age of six. My father had what you would call an old jalopy. We just kind of used that. Or we would use the horses and a cart. So to be here in Heaven and to see anything you want to see—you can get on a bus or a train. There is a group of us who did not know how to drive in that lifetime, so we are not taking our own cars and trying to drive, by any means. But we do get on a bus.*

One of the things I had never seen was the ocean. So we took a bus trip to some place. I don't know if it had a name or if they even have names for their areas. It was a glorious ocean with waves crashing on the beach. The sun was shining. Here you do not have to worry about getting sunburned. We frolicked in the ocean and it was just the right temperature. It was not freezing like some of the oceans in the other world are.

We enjoyed that and are learning that anything you had on Earth, you have in Heaven. It is always at a much more spectacular way. Everything... The only way I can describe it is you know in school and you get a grade—at least my brothers and sisters did—you can either get an A, B, C and so forth. Well, we could say that you could travel and see things that were A+. You don't see any place that you would call a C.

Whenever you take a trip, you know it will be spectacular. And I intend to travel more.

Q: Do you have any idea as to how long you have been in Heaven—when it was that you died?

A: *No, I can guess… The readers can figure it out by seeing who maybe the President was during the dustbowl years (Franklin Delano Roosevelt?). I don't know; I would have to look it up in the library.*

Q: We are coming to the end of our interview time. I have given each of the participants an hour, so it is time to bring this to a close. Do you have any questions that you would like to ask me?

A: *I had not thought that I could ask you a question off hand. An Angel full of Light brought me here. That's all I know. He said I could not go beyond this beam of Light here. We have put a Ring-Pass-Not around this author, so you will know your boundaries. You can only go up to that. If you try to go further, it will push you back.*

Author: the tape ran out so with these 14 pages, I will bring this chapter 9 to a close.

10 MILITARY MAN

03-24-15 Good morning, precious one, we're all set again to bring in Chapter 10, the last of the Entities telling their story. In the next chapter, I will be doing it personally and more or less concluding the book. We, meaning all the rest of the Masters and Angels, are very pleased.

As you know, this last participant is waiting very eagerly to speak with you. He has been instructed to keep everything anonymous and not speak names of that nature to give anything away as to who he and his relatives are. I will step aside now, dear one, and let you enjoy this (6:20 AM).

Hello, I'm ready when you are. Thank you for coming and we will keep this on a simple level, but after I close the interview we can have private time, if you wish. *I would like that very much.*

Alright, I will step aside now and let you tell your story for me and the readers. Give us as much detail as you possibly can. And during the *Question and Answer* period, I will ask you questions so as to give us more detail. Alright, it is up to you.

I am the oldest participant, as you say, of this group who has come (*for the book*). I am honored and I thank you. I was 88 when I died. I am new to Heaven, for I had only died last year (2014). I know that this is not the time to go into my life in its entirety, so I will just touch on that as I bring you up to date.

I was born in a small town in California years ago. I then went to all the different schools; graduated from college. My mother was single by this time. I had a brother.

I had an interesting life which I won't go into. I visited many countries. I had a wife who was very beautiful and I adored. We had 3 daughters.

There came a time in my life that was very sad for me. My wife left me, for I was drinking too much, and she could no longer tolerate that. I could not quit entirely after that, but I certainly got that under control. I met my second wife who brought me much happiness.

She was with me in the hospital room when I died, as was my oldest daughter, her husband, and her two sons. I remember that death as if it were yesterday. My kidneys started failing, shutting down, and I could not breathe with the COPD, and I was no longer able to stand on my legs with the neuropathy. You could say that my body was not in very good shape.

As to my philosophy of life, of course you know up here in Heaven, we've been getting retrained—re-educated. I just wanted to say that in my lifetime I did believe in God. I had, of course, heard all about the Jesus stories but still remained somewhat skeptical. Now since I have met him, I wonder how I could have been so thick-headed, we'll say. But that's another story.

So my dear (*second*) wife brought me to this hospital. I was to the point that every time I had a doctor's appointment, I had to go by ambulance because they had no way of getting me there (*because of my immobility*). So my last doctor's visit was not a very uplifting one. I am unable to give you all of the details, so I can keep this somewhat private. But I am...

I am lying in bed and my philosophy is, *there is a Heaven*. I did not think I would be going to Hell, particularly. I did not lead that much of a derelict life. I never killed anybody; never got into drunken brawls. So I knew I would be going to Heaven, but I did not know how. I had a great deal of fear that I kept from my family.

I guess it was fear of the unknown. I was a Navy pilot and had many adventures during my lifetime—we'll say lots of excitement. But I never experienced much fear. I was just kind of fearless, I guess. But lying in a hospital bed, I was afraid, because death to me was all so unknown. I kind of just pondered my lifetime. When you have 88 years, you have lots to think about. There was stuff I am not too proud of, but I will not go into that.

So I am just lying there and by this time I was not eating very much; sleeping a lot, but not communicating that much to the people who came to visit me. I had 3 daughters. My oldest was able to be with me, but the other 2 lived on the east coast so they were not able to be there. I *did* miss not seeing them for the last time. I hope they know I was thinking of them.

During my youth, I spent a great deal of time in Hawaii, mainly in Maui. So I have left orders in my will to have my ashes scattered over Maui. I had two beloved cats—kitties—who I adored. When they died I was just broken hearted for days. The first Siamese cat, *Tiya*, we took to Greece; I remember she brought joy to us. She died of old age. Then after a while I was given *Nookie*, our last Siamese cat. His name was *Nuoc Mam* after Vietnamese fish sauce, for we had lived there for 3 years. When it came to the time when he had died, I had him cremated and put his ashes into a little box. I have left instructions with my daughter who is executor of my estate that when she spreads my ashes over Maui, I want Nookie's ashes spread right along with mine. I know people will think it's crazy, but it is true—those are my wishes.

So I laid there in my sick bed thinking, *what will death be like? What will happen?* I didn't pay that much attention to it, but my body was already dying as the organs shut down. Pretty soon I was having more trouble breathing so they gave me drugs to help me breathe better and not struggle so. I remember just lying there and thinking, *ok, how's it going to happen? What happens next?*

Then I realized I was no longer able to speak. I heard everything that was going on around me. I wanted to reply, but I just couldn't do it. I wondered if this was how it was when people had strokes or something. I heard everything that was said. My wife was crying on one shoulder and my daughter was crying on the other shoulder; the other people in the room were standing there or sitting and looking very somber. I saw and felt all of that but I could not reply. I do not know how long that lasted. I just laid there.

Then I felt like I was talking to myself. I didn't realize that there was another man there. I did not know his name. I could talk to him and he would talk back. We could communicate! He said to me, *why don't you sit up and we will get out of here.* I said, *how can I do that? I can't move.* He said, *take my hand and I will lift you up.*

I gave him my hand; he gave a gentle pull and the next thing I knew, I was standing by my body. I thought, *well, this is weird.* He said, *you've done it, sir.* I wasn't quite sure why he called me *sir.* I was used to being called *sir* by those under me, but I thought maybe he was a *medical seaman* or someone like that. You get kind of fuzzy, and I was not sure. He said to me, *say your goodbyes; we're leaving now.*

I thought it was kind of strange as I look back on it. I knew... One part of me knew that I was dead and all of this was going on. The other part of me didn't question him. He had this kind of authority, so I just followed him. I went to each person in the room to say *goodbye* to them, but they were still just holding the hand of my body. The man with me said, *they cannot see you, sir. Say goodbye again and why don't we leave?* So I went to each one of them and said *goodbye* and *thank you.* I did not know what else to say. It is very awkward to talk to someone who does not know you are there (*chuckles*)—very awkward. I am laughing now because it seems silly.

There we were and he is taking my hand. The next thing I knew is we seemed to be floating. We went out of the room and down the corridor. It seemed as if we were floating higher and higher. We went up the ceiling and out. The next thing I knew, we were flying like Peter Pan. We were going faster and faster, although it seemed like just a gentle flight. I said to him, *where are we going?* He said, *we are going to Heaven, sir.* I said, *ok, you're the pilot!*

I have no recollection of a tunnel or anything like that. One minute we were in the hospital room on Earth and the next minute I knew I was in what is known as *Heaven*, which was a huge shock for me. It was entirely different from anything that I had imagined. It's literally another world. You've got Earth and then you have Heaven—two worlds! I just remember thinking, *this is fascinating. I can hardly wait to get a plane and fly around it—see it from the sky.*

So I turned to this man and asked, *what is your name?* He said, *I am your Guardian Angel.* By this time I was ready to go along with what anyone said. I said, *I am so-and-so.* He said, *yes, I know, sir.* Again he took my hand, and we approached this building that was just huge. I asked, *are you taking me to another hospital?*

(Oh, I want to back up a bit. I left my body dead with my wife and my daughter holding my hands. And yet I look just like that body. I am not that decrepit; I am walking just fine; my hair is still grey. I seem to float more than I actually walk.) My Guardian Angel took me into this building which he said was a *Care Center*. He led me to a room. I thought, *well, don't you go to the desk, register and sign in—you know all that stuff?* Of course, he was reading my mind, which I found out later that he could do. He said, *no, that is not necessary. They know you are here. The Angels have a way of communicating so that everyone knows that you are here.*

So again I just went along with it. All my life, you see, I just followed orders (*Navy*). This was no different. *Come here, sir,* and I went. He took me to this very pleasant room. It was painted in a soft shade of blue. That was one of my favorite colors.

Here was this bed that didn't look like a hospital bed at all—just a nice bed with a lot of pillows. There was a comfy chair. My Angel said, *alright, you can take off that hospital gown now.* I looked at myself and was aghast that I had still been roaming around in that hospital gown, flapping free in the back. He just smiled and said, *you can take that off and climb into bed here. You've had a long journey and it is time to just rest. This Care Center will heal you so that your body will no longer have those ailments.*

I said, *they'll heal everything so that I can breathe? I am walking better, but all of that will be healed?* He said, *yes sir; lie down now and rest.* So I yanked the hospital gown off and climbed into bed. It actually felt wonderful. I was still thinking about those I had left behind, but I had traveled so much (*during my lifetime*) that I was still in that category: *you are there and I am here.*

I apparently went to sleep or passed out or something. The next thing I knew, I was awake again. The sun was shining through the window. My Angel was still there. He said, *good morning, sir.* I said *good morning* back. He asked me how I felt. I told him I felt great. He said, *your body was healed.* I said, *oh thank God for that.* He said, *yes, thank Him for that.*

Alright sir, now we need to go to another building. I got up and saw I had on this green robe. I wondered how that happened. Apparently Angels read your mind, for he said, *that was put on you after they had healed your body.* I took him at his word. I felt alright so I must have been healed. I could breathe so that was no longer a problem. I could walk so that problem was fixed. So actually I was feeling pretty good.

I asked, *is there a mirror around here so I can see what I look like?* He said, *over there by the sink.* I walked to the mirror and looked at me. I looked just like I had looked, but I seemed a speck younger. I did not look as tired. I noticed that I stood up straighter, still had my grey hair and that military haircut which everyone hated but me. It was so comfortable. I just looked at myself and thought, *hmm, I don't look that much different, but I sure feel different.* I know that my thinking was clearer, but it all was kind of receding at the same time (*thoughts of Earth*).

The Angel said again, *alright, we're going to go to another building.* We went to this building that was just a little ways away and went in. There were all of these people looking at movie screens. I did not know quite what was going on, but then I had kind of a nagging thought in my head. *Oh, I wonder if this is where you get your review.* I had always heard that there would be a review but had not paid that much attention to that. *Oh boy, this is going to be a longgg day!*

He led me to this large screen and said, *ok sir, sit down and you will get to look at your life.* I sat down and it started way back when I was a baby, which surprised me. My mother was quite beautiful. She was a good mother.

So I looked at—you know when you live to be 88 there is just one experience after the other. I felt it all; saw it all; felt it all. What can I say? You are flooded with feelings—just flooded. I know as I went through the different periods of my life, it seemed as if the movie went into slow motion so you got the whole benefit of that and would not miss a thing.

I saw all of my school years, then college, then my marriage to my beautiful wife. We had our children, my career—it went on and on. I experienced the happiness I felt with each of my babies and how much fun they were. I played games with them, carried them around on my 6' 4" shoulders. I really enjoyed that part of it (*review*). I cannot describe each section of those 88 years. As I say, some of it I delighted in and other parts I was not quite so proud of.

It seemed as if I sat there for 88 years just watching me live those 88 years (*chuckles*). I came to the end of the review and saw me lying in the hospital room—or wherever it was—and they (*relatives*) were crying. I felt sad for them because I did not want to part from them either. But it is all part of life, isn't it? We have heard so often that what we can count on is death and taxes. So that was it! That was the end to my 88 years.

The screen turned off and I sat there sort of numbed out. My Angel let me stay there a while in thought then he said, *can I bring you anything, sir? Would you like something?* I said, *no, I'm alright*. I got up and was surprised at my agility in springing up out of the chair. I had not done that for years. I said, *alright, now what do I do?* He said, *I am going to take you to another area; you will find many people there. They all died about the same time that you did and they are at the level that you are. So you do not have to worry about there being kids or ancient ones there. Everybody is in the same boat, shall we say. You will know what I mean when we get there.*

He took me to this room. I must say it was crowded. Everyone was speaking at once. Some were older than I; some were younger. I just went in and thought *I better introduce myself.* I went to different people and said, *hello, how did you get here*—you know stuff like that, like you would talk at a cocktail party, except none of us had had any drinks.

Very shortly this man came in; he introduced himself as the *facilitator of this group*, as he put it. Since my former wife had gotten her degrees in psychology, I wasn't too happy about all of that. But I kept my mouth shut and thought, *ok, I will see what he has to say, but if I don't like it, I will just leave.* I was pretty used to doing what I wanted, you know. When you are in the military at a certain rank, you can just leave and go someplace else if you don't like where you are. But he surprised me, actually. He greeted us and made sure we all knew we were dead, which I was sort of amazed at. I guess some people don't know they are dead. Then he made sure we all knew we had made it to Heaven. That was considered kind of a joke, so to speak. So the facilitator starts talking. He went around and asked how different people died. That was interesting. You don't know all the different ways people die. Then he asked how many had had the tunnel experience. Maybe half raised their hands. Like me, I didn't, so that was discussed. Not everybody arrives in Heaven through the tunnel. So he talked about that.

By this time he adjourned. I guess for the first time they know everyone has just had their life review so they don't spend that much time—I won't say socializing—but they won't spend that much time… whatever that group is called. We were told we would meet there again the next day.

My Guardian Angel was right there and he said, *alright, sir, we are now going to find accommodations for you.* I was interested in that. Hmm, what kind of accommodations does Heaven have? He also said, *I know you must be hungry so we will also go to the...* He called it the *Mess Hall* (a military term). I thought to myself, *oh Lord, I hope it is not all full.*

Anyway, I followed him; he took me to this... I don't quite know how to explain it. He took me to this house, actually. It was a large house with different rooms. Actually, it reminded me of a fraternity house, except it was furnished much nicer. There were different floors. He said, *do you want to be upstairs or downstairs?* I said, *I would like to be upstairs because I don't want to have people clomping over the top of my head.*

There was an elevator; we got in and it went swiftly up to the next floor. He took me to this room. I said, *well, how do we know what room we've got?* He said, *you will know. It will have your name on the door.* I thought, *oh, ok.* The room wasn't half bad. It was like a very nice room that one would find in a very nice hotel. It even had a television screen. I hadn't thought of Heaven having television. There was a small bathroom with a shower but there wasn't any toilet.

I thought, *oh no, don't tell me there is going to be a communal place.* Again he (*Angel*) could read my mind. He just said, *you won't need a toilet, sir.* I didn't quite get it, but I was starting to feel tired and didn't want to argue with him. He said, *will this room be satisfactory for you?* I said, *oh yeah, this is fine.* He said, *alright, why don't we go to the Dining Hall?* Actually, since this house was quite large, there was a dining room, shall we say. All along one wall was all the food. I found that I was hungrier than I realized.

I filled up my plate, went over to this table and pretty soon other people came over too. I noticed there weren't any women, so I guess this was a man's house. The Angel said, *yes it is.* So I sat and chit-chatted with the other guys. The Angels just kind of—they all had one too—they just kind of melted into the background.

I ate and that's about it; I don't know what else to tell you. So I guess I will leave it up to you at this time. You wanted to ask questions, you said. *Yes.*

Questions (Q) and Answers (A)

Q: You described what you looked like, but are you still in your eighties? (*He could be in his thirties.*)

A: *I am not quite sure now. My hands seem to look a little younger.*

Q: When you were in your group, did the facilitator talk about life contracts and things of that nature?

A: *Not at that time, but he did later on. Each of us examined the contracts that we had. I saw that everything I had done was on that contract. I was to marry twice and I did. I was to have 3 children and I did. I was to lead a military life and I did. So I pretty much had done everything on my contract. Some of it kind of surprised me, for I did not know I was supposed to have a second wife until it happened. But I see now that my first wife had followed the contract and I rebelled against that for a long time, for which I am sorry.*

Q: Have you seen your pets, your kitty-cats again?

A: *Not yet, but I know we will be seeing where the animals are. I had asked about that and my dear kitties are waiting for me, I was told. They could even be in my room when I get back.*

Q: Did any relatives meet you, like your mother or grandparents or anything like that?

A: *I have yet to see them. I am looking forward to that but I haven't seen them yet.*

Q: You have not been dead all that long—just a few months. So you haven't met any of your past military friends or any one like that either?

A*: No, I have concentrated on just... They have this term* retrained. *So I am concentrating on where I went wrong in my belief systems and I am changing those. And I am not ready yet to meet all the past relatives or friends. They seem very distant to me, and I am not pulled to see them yet. I know there will come a time when I will, but it is not my focus right now.*

Q: I am going to be asking some of the questions I have asked everyone else. When you had your life review or when you discussed your contracts in your group, did you talk about your purpose in this last lifetime? What was that purpose?

A: *I had different purposes. I did not have just one. I had a purpose in deepening my heart. That very definitely was one. Another purpose was... You see, I was a flyer and there was a purpose in that vocation. It was to be able to meet the situations with the weather. I guess it was one of courage and determination for that lifetime. I flew a great deal, so I had to be able to do that.*

Q: Did you talk about reincarnation?

A: *We spoke about it briefly in that first meeting. It has been several months since then, so we have talked more about reincarnation. Yes, I plan to do that. It has not been set up as to whom I will meet. That will all be done as it gets closer to the time that I will incarnate. Since I have just died, so to speak, I am in no rush to get back. There is too much to learn here.*

Q: You said you were being *retrained*. What are you being retrained about?

A: *I had some weird beliefs about the medical field and psychology, Heaven and Jesus and all of that. So all that is part of the retraining— also religion. I was never baptized in that lifetime, and I am finding that that is a choice and is not a command. That surprised me.*

Q: Have you met any of the Ascended Masters?

A: *Well, if you mean by Ascended—very high lighted ones—I have met the one you call Jeshua. He is the one I am finding out is connected with you, which surprised me. And he is the one who brought me to you.*

Q: Some of the participants talked about the pearly gates, but most had not seen them. Did you see any pearly gates and streets of gold as described in the Bible?

A: *No, that was all in a person's imagination, we were told and they did not exist.*

Q: Did you believe in a Hell?

A: *Oh yeah! You can't be a military man without believing in Hell. I was just thankful that my life was exemplary enough so that I went to Heaven instead.*

Q: Did you attend your own funeral or memorial?

A: *No, I did not wish that to happen. My girls are going to spread my ashes and that has not been done yet. So you see some of the questions you asked the other participants really do not relate to me.*

Q: Yes, I am finding that out. How about traveling? Have you traveled quite a bit since you have been in Heaven?

A: *That is one of the first things I did when I heard you could go by bus, train or by airplane. I said, how do you get an airplane? They told me all about it. It is very similar to Earth. You go and request a plane. They question you just a bit as to what your training is and what kind of plane do you want. I told them.*

Q: Do you have to file a flight plan if you are going to take a plane out?

A: *Umm, it's different up here. The flight plan is to give you a destination since you do not know where you are going—suggestions: you can go here or you can go there. In that way we file a flight plan. Our Angel always goes with us, so we can't get lost. The planes don't crash. But interestingly enough, you can set up ahead of time if you want to practice flying in stormy weather.*

You can request you want a flight where you will be in thunderclouds and things like that so you can practice with your airplane. I remember those horrendous thunderheads we had to go through when we entered Vietnam from the Philippines. As we came to the coast of Vietnam, the thunderheads were so high, I knew it was always going to be a thrill to fly my plane through that.

I did not realize at the time, but I was saying a prayer: ok, God get me through this. *Sometimes I had my wife as a passenger in the tail of the plane. She was petrified, although she tried to do everything to keep herself calm, even as to painting her toenails as we bumped along.*

So I have been flying a lot here. It is an absolute joy for me. I fly whenever I can. I am getting more skilled at getting through these very challenging flights. So I have traveled quite a bit. I am noting that everything there is on Earth, like lakes, oceans, jungles, deserts, mountains, forests, are on Heaven. Everything you have on Earth, you have on Heaven as far as the things I have just mentioned. So it is a great pleasure. I have flown to each coast, shall we say. I don't go to the jungle. I do not like that particularly, but someday I may. So yes, I have traveled quite a bit and yes, I file a flight plan simply because it gives you a destination. Otherwise you do not know where you are going.

Q: Some people may have a job of some kind with a title for it like a baker or something of that nature. Do you do anything like that—a job that occupies your time?

A: *I have not run into being bored. There is always something to do, some place to go. There are people galore to talk to or no one to talk to. It is whatever you want. You can eat when you want or not eat. I notice I am eating less. I still enjoy cooking, so I have been to the culinary department leaning how to cook different things. I enjoyed cooking when I had my life.*

Let's see...what else—a job. Uh, I have not been assigned to one. I think when it comes to my having a job it will have something to do with maybe flight school. You would be surprised how many people want to learn how to fly, especially women who want to learn how to fly. I don't have it yet, but I know l will always have a job open for me if I wish at flight school.

Q: I have a friend who wanted to know… First of all she asked what you do when you get to Heaven. Do you feel fulfilled? Do you feel like you have a reason to be?

A: *It's funny because I thought about those same things as I was lying in that hospital bed. I thought,* God, what is it going to be like? *Since I had a lot of trepidation, I did not know. But to answer her question, what do you do when you get to Heaven, you start exploring. You can go to any place that you want to go to because you can think it and you are there. Or if you want to drive a car you can do that.*

Your friend asked if you would feel fulfilled. Yes, actually, I feel quite fulfilled. I imagine it is up to the individual. I think those who never had a particular passion for their work on Earth, they may not feel fulfilled. But that is just my supposition. For me, I feel quite fulfilled; I am excited. There are things to do all of the time.

As far as my reason for being… that is very deep and would be something to discuss with the facilitator or with our Angel. I know on a soul level we are to grow. My wife of many years was wiser than I was and she knew these things before I did. She is still alive. I did not learn any of this until I died, so it is to your advantage to study these New Age thoughts which I would have poo-pooed when I was alive. But it is to your advantage to do so because the soul is evolving and it is growing. The amazing thing is you don't know that you are growing. When you are having so much pleasure at what you are doing and learning so much, that is all part of soul growth. You are growing whether you realize it or not. I am very excited about it all.

Q: It sounds like it; that's really fun for you. Well, we are almost out of time for this interview. Stay afterwards and we can talk about personal things. I thank you for coming. Is there a question you would like to ask me? I have asked that of everyone who has participated and have given them that opportunity if they wished.

A: *That surprises me just a bit. I wasn't expecting that. Let's see—what I would like to ask you, the author of this book—does writing books fulfill you? Is that your purpose?*

Q: I haven't been asked that before either, but I can say yes, it does fulfill me and yes, that is one of my purposes. So with that, we will end our interview and I thank you for coming and may many blessings be yours when you reincarnate and start your new life.

A: *Thank you very much; this has been a great adventure. I count it as right up there among my flying trips. I have flown to you, so I appreciate that.*

You are welcome; I am very appreciative of your coming. So I will end this interview for now. We will say over and out (*flyers signing off*).

That's as good as any. Bye.

Bye. (7:45 AM)

Alright, dear one, I am Jeshua. You have lots to write up and the next time you sit, I will be the next and last participant.

Yes, Jeshua, thank you so much.

You are welcome, dear one. Namaste.

Namaste.

11 ASCENDED MASTER-MAN

O3-28-15 *Saturday, 7:05 AM. Good morning, my precious one. We are all set to go on Chapter 11. I am the Ascended Master known as* Sananda *and this will be my chapter.*

I do not need to go back to my birth, for that is what we shall say is history at this time. It is death that this book is about; therefore, I shall speak of mine. I did not have a death similar to the other participants of this book, but it was quite significant to me. I shall be as specific as I can.

Humanity is fed the story of my body being dragged through the streets carrying a cross. That dear friends, shockingly, did *not* happen. I was *not* put on the cross. I was *not* crucified on the cross.*** I ascended willingly. I laid my body down and died. It was as simple as that.

As you read this chapter, you readers need to set aside all the biblical quotations, all the biblical stories, because so many of them are just that—stories, like the Grimms' Fairy Tales; they are not true.

When it came time for me to die, I was in my light body, we will say... Well, that is confusing; let me back up. You have read the other participants' stories of how they had slipped out of their body and went whooshing up to Heaven.

There came a time in my life when I was persecuted. The Romans did wish to kill me, so I decided I would do it my way. I conferred with different relatives and since we are making this book anonymous, I will not name them. I then went privately to a cave of my uncle's.

I had had many Initiations in Egypt where I learned how to still my body for 3 days at a time and then come back.* I decided if I stayed around the Romans much longer, they would grab me and crucify me as they did other people because that was their way of killing people.

Therefore, in the dead of night—and remember (*readers*) keep your thoughts out of the Bible because so much of it is not true—in the dead of night, we, my beloved wife and others went to the tomb of my uncle.

I laid down and went into the sleep that I had learned how to induce (*altered state of consciousness*) while in Egypt. I laid there after having said goodbye to those who were with me. I laid there and asked my Higher Self to help me on my journey; that I wished to vacate my body permanently.

There was no argument, for they knew more about it than I did and knew that my staying there would be a very difficult, painful time for me. Therefore, I put myself in this deep sleep and asked *my* guides and *my* angels to not awaken me until my body had died.

I slept for those many hours. I stilled the organs in my body; I commanded my body to stop breathing. I released my hold on my body. (So many people hang on and I did not wish to do that.) I remember saying the words, *I am ready to leave.* I thanked my body, for it was a magnificent body with many abilities. The next thing I remember when I released—the participants talk about a whoosh—I felt this whoosh. I seemed to be just propelled out of the body. There was my Guardian

Angel with me. We shot through the cave ceiling and just kept going. I must say it was kind of a shocking experience, for I was in, we'll say, the astral body, shooting straight up through this portal.

What was interesting to me as I look back on it was I was able to carry on a conversation with my Angel. I guess I can liken it to your spaceships that are traveling at a tremendous speed and yet the astronauts feel like they are just floating. The whooshing feeling did not last, but I knew I was moving. I had a robe on and could see it was moving with me.

I came to this world I knew as Heaven. Heaven was a delight for me. I saw no pearly gates, for that was not my belief. My Angel did take me to the Care Center. It seems as if everyone goes to the Care Center on his/her arrival. They are taken into a room and a bed, told to take off their robe and climb into bed. I did so and felt myself feeling sleepy, which surprised me. My Angel said, *it is the energy, Master; it's the energy.* I remember feeling surprised that he had called me *Master,* but then they called me that on Earth, too.

I got into bed and the next thing I knew, I was asleep. During that time, they had healed my body. I had some of the cuts and bruises on me from the brutal questioning by the Romans. I did *not* have the crown of thorns. That was all made up by the scribes, but when anyone was interrogated and did not give the answer that they, the interrogators, were looking for, you got slapped around. They used a whip more often than not. They put you into the category of being a slave and whipped you if you did not answer or do what they had asked. My body did have some of those repercussions that needed to be healed.

Then when I awoke, I too had on a new robe—the "*mantle of greatness.*"** It was a robe of many colors, actually—green for healing, blue for peace, (*pink for love*), yellow and gold. It was quite beautiful.

Then my Angel said, *now Master, are you feeling better?* I replied, *of course I am; who wouldn't? That was quite an experience.* He said, *yes.* Then he took me to the building that had the computers and movie screens, and I sat and I watched the review of my life. This shocks many people, for they do not expect that I would (*have a review*). But we all have a time when we need to look back on our actions and what other people felt about us because of our actions. So I sat and watched mine.

I saw where I was arrogant at times and how that arrogance had emotionally wounded people. I did not like that about myself. I sat there—I don't know how long a time it was—and saw my life. Then the movie went blank; I stood up and said, *alright, Angel, where do we go next?* He said, *I am going to take you to a room where there are others who died about the same time as you did.*

We went into the room. There were not a great many people there, but amazingly, they were *all* Masters. They were from all races and colors of skin. I had not thought that much about it, but I certainly was not the only one. The facilitator came in and talked about retraining. He went around the room and we described our different deaths. Some of the Masters had been beaten to death. There were some who had been hung on a tree and left to die. But history does not record those. Therefore, we heard the way different people had died. We told our personal stories of what it was like watching the review. Others had different—I won't call it *failings*—but parts of their emotional makeup that needed retraining.

One thing I noticed was we were all more or less on the same level. As I have listened to the different stories that the participants have told for this book, it is obvious that the Care Center and the room where the facilitator helps to retrain us are on different levels—different dimensions—so we never saw the new people who came in. You can liken it to school. There would be people in kindergarten, middle grades, high school, college, and advanced learning (*post graduates*). And each one of those grades would be on a different level. We were on this level for Masters.

When the facilitator had finished what he was talking about for that period, my Angel (I don't know about the others) said, *alright, Master, now we are going to visit your God.* I was kind of shocked, for this Luminescent was so high above me, I had not thought of meeting him so soon.

My Angel took me... I don't know how to explain this. You could say it was an elevator, but it was more than that. He said, *now just think of where you would like to go. Think of being in front of Him.* I said it in a prayer, actually. Before I knew it, there I was in front of this magnificent God—Luminescent. He knew his Light was too bright for most of us for the first time, so he dimmed his Light just a bit so as not to blind us. Readers, it would be like a light bulb that has different wattages. He just dimmed his Light down to a lower wattage.

I went to him and knelt. His energy was love and it was overwhelming, so I knelt (*kind of fell to my knees*). He touched me in some way—I do not know how—and he said, *no, Sananda, you no longer need to kneel before me. We are one.* He stared or looked into my eyes and I felt myself engulfed into him. He said to me, *you will now be known as an Ascended Master, for you have ascended. You may travel to any place that you wish. You may travel to different worlds, different Universes and know that I will always be with you.* I felt overwhelmed. I don't know how, but again I found myself in a beautiful area. It was like what one would call an *estate* of some kind. My Angel told me, *this is your sanctuary. You may decorate it in any way that you wish, but this is yours.*

I can't think of anything else to say at this time. I know with the others you asked questions. So if you would like to ask me questions, I am ready.

Alright, some of the questions might not fit you, but you can always tell me if they don't (*chuckles*).

Questions (Q) and Answers (A)

Q: How old were you when you died?

A: *That is correctly told; I was 33.*

Q: What form do you have now?

A: *I take any form that I wish. I am most comfortable as pure energy— pure spirit.*

Q: Did you have a pre-birth contract?

A: *I did; I was not able to finish that contract because I had to leave prematurely. If I had not left, I would have been crucified and I had no desire for that experience.*

Q: What was your purpose in that lifetime?

A: *Actually I had more than one. People usually do not realize that they usually have more than one purpose. My purpose was to spread love throughout humanity. I was not able to complete that mission. Another purpose was my beloved wife and I were changing the DNA structure of humanity. We were not able to complete that either.*

Q: Now that you have told us about Heaven, what *is* the size of Heaven? We have one, the Military-Man, who tells us he is flying around it, but what is the size of Heaven?

A: *You could say that Heaven is another world, a planet, and there are all sizes, as you know. To simplify it, I can say that Heaven is a world of many levels which you can say are* dimensions. *And no, I will not say how many dimensions. Just say, as far as you can count.*

Q: So many of the readers have different concepts of Heaven, so some of these questions are to help them understand it a bit more. Is there a time limit as to how long a Being can remain in Heaven?

A: *The time limit is regulated by the Entity's Over-soul. Some Beings would like to stay there forever. But then, you see, their soul is not evolving. They always have their Angel with them. They always have their facilitator to talk to. So when it gets to the point when the Over-soul says,* OK, we've got to get him/her motivated to return to Earth to continue his/her growth... *in that way it is like a parent telling them,* alright, you've got to get back to Earth and back to school.

Q: Many people believe in Hell; so I am asking is there a place in Heaven to fulfill that expectation or is it still totally in one's imagination?

A: *Hell, as you know, is an illusion, but the person can create that illusion, so there* could *be a Hell. And maybe there is a person right next to him that also believes in a Hell, so then they could be in that same Hell. Before you know it, everyone who believes in Hell has a Hell to go to, but it still is an illusion. When you no longer believe in that illusion, you leave it. I could say* yes, *there is an area and* no, *there isn't* (chuckles) *because it is still an illusion. Some parts of it are fairly grim and others are not. But it is still Hell and it is still an illusion that somebody started because that was his/her belief system. Does that make sense to you?* Yes.

Q: Does your Monad have strings of consciousness in Beings on Earth now?

A: *Yes, actually, I have people that I have my consciousness in. I will not say who they are or how many, but yes, we do that.*

Q: When you went to your group, did you have beliefs that you had to retrain?

A: *Not in the way you are implying. I believed in the ability of man-kind, woman-kind, to open their hearts and to have love and be loved. That belief system was very strong. So I cannot say that that had to be retrained. My arrogance was not a belief system. It was the youth of me at times thinking I knew everything. And I did not. All I can say is you know what I mean* (chuckles). *Yep, I do.*

Q: It is frequently said that when one dies, there are always past relatives who come to greet them, yet with the 10 I have interviewed, nobody has come to greet them yet, although they have seen some of them. Did you have any friends or relatives greet you as you came to Heaven?

A: *No, not in that sense, but I, too, have since seen them, of course. We'll say since it has been thousands of years ago, at that time period I did see some of the people—not so much relatives—who had influenced my beliefs, we'll say, up to that time.*

Q: I cannot think of any more questions that would be apropos at this time, but I have asked all the other participants if they had a question for me. So I will ask you the same thing: do you have a question for me?

A: *I had anticipated that and yes, I am not going to let you go Scot-free without my asking you a question. My question is do you love yourself?*

Oh, boy, might have known—back to love! (*Chuckles*)

Yes, dearest one.

At times I love myself, yes. At other times—I think I will say it is like parents with a child. They love the child, but there are times when they don't like that child. That is how I feel about myself. At times I don't like myself.

I will accept that answer.

Q: We are coming to the end of this interview, so I will ask you if you have any last words for our readers.

A: *Dearest readers, some of my story will shock your belief systems; I know that. But keep an open mind. Always be flexible. I can say that almost nothing is—we'll use that term—black or white. There is always some gray in between. So the same applies with your belief systems.*

Know that the subject you think is so absolute probably is not. There could be times when it will not be. So keep that in mind. Be flexible. Everything is changing. The energy is always changing. The Luminescent of this Universe is always pouring energy into this world. So how could there not be change? So your belief systems, readers, most likely need to change. With that, I will ask this author if she feels complete.

Yes, and this interview is closed.

Thank you, my precious author. Until we meet again, which is never far away, since I am—I reside within you.

May I reiterate with you the story you told us?

Of course.

So you were not crucified; you did not carry the cross?

NO.

You were whipped by the Romans as they interrogated you?

YES.

You chose when to die and you went to your uncle's tomb and practiced what you had learned in the Initiations in Egypt?

YES.

You stilled your body and commanded it to release you and to die?

YES.

You had an Angel with you and you whooshed to Heaven when you died?

YES.

You went to the Care Center to have your whipping cuts and bruises healed?

YES, and some of my organs.

You then woke up and had a beautiful, colorful robe on?

YES.

You went to the review room and sat there just like everyone else does and had the review of your life?

YES.

After that you went to what I call the *Group Process* room?

YES.

Your facilitator talked with other people there?

YES, most of the other participants had around 40-50 people in their room.

I take it your room did not have that many?

YES, that is true. There were not that many Masters there. I would say there were around a dozen.

Then after the facilitator closed that class for that time, did you keep meeting there?

YES, we did go back, but not many times. It was mainly to help us with the questionings we may have had in our review and to help us with any areas within ourselves that were not correct. For me, it was mainly the arrogance of youth.

Your Angel guide took you to God?

YES.

Did he sit on a throne?

He was sitting, but his Light was so brilliant I did not pay that much attention as to what his throne looked like. Then he dimmed his Light just a bit so I could see him. By this time he had taken a form, so I was able to see his eyes. It seemed as if I was... I just drowned into them. Or we could say he pulled me into them. I do not know how long I was with him. We talked of many things. We spoke of what was needed for humanity.

Then you came back to Earth?

YES, but I was in what is called a light-body. *The best I can say is it was a form but it was mostly Light. So I had (another life) then with my wife for a while. Then I did go to the Himalayas—the Far East—to India. In that region after many of your Earth years, I ascended once again.*

Do you see the other Ascended Masters often?

YES, there are various councils. Each council has a purpose. So I am always in contact with the Masters as we guide humanity on Earth.

I am dedicated to helping people to raise their consciousness so that Earth can raise her consciousness. When there is a barrel of muck, that has to be cleaned out so that cleaner—I am looking at a barrel of apples, shall we say? All the spoiled, rotting apples must be cleaned out, so that the fresh, new ones can reside and not contaminate the others. Of course, that is a metaphor for all (governments) must be cleaned.

I am working closely with the different countries of the world. Since you are in America, I am involved in helping those people. I work a great deal with the government of America. And to use our metaphor of the barrel of rotten apples, I will say that many of those apples in that government need to be picked out, pulled out, for they are contaminating the whole concept of democracy.

We are getting away from the subject of this book, so I will now step aside. But readers, if you have enjoyed this book and want more, we are going to have Vol.II, and we are going to have women as subjects, shall we say—so they can tell their death stories.

Thank you so much, Lord Sananda. *Now* this interview is closed!

Thank you, precious one; thank you. (8:15 AM)

*Readers, never try this for Jesus had special training. Pharaohs laid in their sarcophagus for 3 days in their attempt to become a "Winged Pharaoh." Not all of them survived.

**The *"mantle of greatness"* is achieved by a soul who has reached a certain level in its expansion. All souls exist on a level of maturity on different levels of awareness. The colors of the mantle reflect the pure essence of the soul.

***Author: In the book: <u>And Then God Said… Then I Said… Then He Said, Vol. One</u> by Celestial Blue Star and David of Arcturus and Suzy Ward (2008), they wrote:

"The FACT is that Jesus was never put on a cross, so there was no crucifixion or resurrection." (pg. 30)

<u>*www.awakenedhearts.com*</u>

EPILOGUE

O3-31-15. This book is finished! I can hardly believe I wrote it in two months!

I was working on Chapter 8 when it became clear to me that all of my subjects were male. I was to write Volume II from the female perspective also! I ran this by Jeshua and he agreed—in fact he had already chosen the next 10 women. Unbelievable! What a novel idea.

These ten men who have come forth so willingly to tell their stories were a delight to me from the get-go. And as they described their experiences in Heaven, it filled in the blank spots that I had not known—for example, check out an airplane and go explore!

I must admit channeling Sananda's chapter was somewhat of a challenge for me. The information he was giving me was outside the box that humanity had placed him in. It was quite controversial to the present religious beliefs. I kept thinking, *wow, and wait until they have their reviews. There's going to be a lot of retraining needed!*

Readers, you have now read the book. Click on your flexibility button and see if your beliefs need some tweaking! Jesus/Jeshua/Sananda was

NOT crucified? He sat in front of the screens and viewed *his* life? Unbelievable!

I invite your comments, with much love, Chako.

AZchako@aol.com & www.Godumentary.com/chako

GOD'S CHILDREN

It has been known down through the ages that as souls came into their bodies, there would be trials and tribulations that they would have to experience. Some of these souls were very advanced; some were just learning; some were passing from one season to another, for as God has told us the souls go through their own seasons: Spring, Summer, Fall, and Winter.

Each season is a learning for the soul. The souls take bodies in order to learn their lessons and so they can advance to another level in that season or they can advance forward to the next season.

The souls are from all walks of life. Some have been greatly educated, others are illiterate in many ways. Either way becomes a learning experience. You have heard many times readers, that the soul is having a spiritual learning experience in its body.

How many of these experiences had to do with religions? Since my name of *Jesus* has been associated with Christianity I will speak on that. Christianity is not the guiding light that it was purported to be. When you think of it, the various religions were set up; no matter what the religion, there were always those to control it and there were those to lift it up or tear it down.

Christianity had its dark period. During the Inquisitions, there would be a panel of people who would judge a woman who just happened to be what is known as *psychic*. Therefore, these so called saints who sat on the board to judge her called her a *witch*. You have all heard about the witch-hunts that took place in America, many in Salem, Massachusetts. All of this was distorted thinking, dear readers.

I wish to speak about what I call *in my day*. In my day, back some 2,000 years ago now, Christianity was not born yet. You have heard about the different stories of the Israelites, Moses, and Abraham. Some of those biblical stories were correct. Some were not, but those people who called themselves *Fundamentalists* (religious fanatics) always felt that they were right.

Long ago before the religions were born, there were always sects of people with particular ideas. They always had a sense that there was someone higher than themselves. The term we use is *God*. The Gods themselves use the term *Luminescent*. There were these Luminescents that created the Universes, created the worlds; created the people—the souls.

Therefore, a soul of long ago came in with the programming it had received already from its parents. Oddly enough, those parents who you would call illiterate, similar to some of the mountain people of long ago, did not know how to write and so they made an X mark. They knew not how to read but they had an oral history that they passed on. Therefore, they kept their particular beliefs on going. Since they did not have the news media to dilute any of their pure beliefs, they were many times in truth closer to God than those in stylized religions.

There was a man who you called St. Paul. He used to walk miles or rode a horse for miles preaching his concept which grew into the religion, *Christianity*, which is a play on words: the Christ—Christ-ianity.

What is sad is that while they had a smattering of truth, each sect became diluted when all the egos began to control it—controlled the words—*this is what was said.*

A mountain woman was closer to God as she walked through the meadows, as she walked through the forest picking out medicinal leaves, roots, and berries as a healer. She knew what she was doing. She just felt it, but with the lack of education, she did not make it into a dogma; did not put it into words. People of her village and other villages would come to her for they felt she was a healer and they trusted her. When they were healed, the people knew she spoke truth.

The mountain people were very forth right. They did not put on what is called *airs* in order to appear different. They were what they were. All the people were more or less the same. They had their very rustic cabins and lived off the land. Their downfall, however, was when they learned how to make liquor from the grains. Then pretty soon alcoholism became the norm.

If you look back in history, you can see the gradual decline of peoples. One wonders what causes this decline. Then a scholar noted and made the correlation: the people had learned how to make liquor. Then they learned how to sell it, so if people did not know how to make it, they could always buy it. Since most people had little money in those days, they bartered and made a trade for alcoholism.

You readers may be wondering what I am leading up to. But you can see the different gradations of the soul—what Blue Star and God call the *Seasons of the Soul*. For so many in those earlier days, the soul was in its *Springtime*, learning by trial and error. Then after the soul was able to make some strides in that, it graduated to the next level of *Summer of the Soul*. The lessons became more difficult. They were educated now. They had to find ways to go to school, go on to college and obtain their degrees so that they would have more knowledge. This knowledge did not always turn into wisdom, but they learned of that after they had died and dropped their body and had their review.

With the knowledge, you see, their egos became stronger. They learned how to manipulate, control, and how to dominate. The woman was discarded as the lesser God. It was a patriarchic society. Women turned over their autonomy to the man. They became subservient, even as late as 50 years or so ago. A woman went to college with the goal to find her husband, get married and have his children. It was not go to college, find a vocation and go to work, although many gradually through the years did work outside the home. But they gave over their rights to a man; it truly became a *rite of passage*. They gave their autonomy to their husband. It was the way of the world, the *Summer Season of Souls*.

The souls then graduated to the *Fall Season of the Soul*. Now they are smarter and more educated, but their compassion was lacking. They had lost their ability to love deeply. Their heart was shallow for they had lost their autonomy. Love became sex. Love lost its deeper meaning, for sex always came first, then love. In the Fall Season of a Soul they fought each other in the work place. It was always climbing on each other's back to get to the top. They stole; they cursed their fellow workers.

They religiously went to church, for it was the thing to do, and they were controlled by their church. Some of the sects told them how to dress; whether you could have dances in the church. All the religions today would probably say that dancing is fine because no one does slow dancing any more. There is no coming together of that caring quality as you gently hold your partner, loving her in a caring way.

The Fall Season for a Soul has many trials and tribulations. It is honing the soul. If the soul is lacking in compassion, it will opt to have many experiences where there are painful losses of all kinds: painful loss of a pet; painful loss of a job; painful loss of relatives, spouses and children. The deeper the pain the more sorrow and hence the overture for the awakening of the heart at a deeper level.

There are always those who turn to alcohol to deaden the pain so that they do not have to feel it. In that way, they have stopped the growth of their heart. The heart does not feel compassion then for it is now drowning in its victimhood where there is only anger.

In the corporate world as people climb the ladder, or climb each other's shoulders and step on the person below them, they have lost their compassion also; they have lost the caring. The Fall Season for the Soul is hard work. All the lessons that it needs for its own growth are multiplied. If the task was difficult for a Spring or Summer Soul, it could now be 3 times as difficult—exponentially for the Fall Soul. Many times the lessons are the same. It is just the severity and the length of time to experience these losses that has changed.

Some souls in their Fall Season try the game of distancing themselves from a situation, hoping that this would be the way to put it all behind him or herself. *I will distance myself so I will not have to see you and feel the pain that you have put me through,* taking no ownership, no responsibility. This is different from distancing oneself from an <u>energy</u> that is no longer compatible for you. The distance I am speaking of is where the soul does not want to interact with someone because it is too emotionally painful and it is easier to just not deal with the situation.

The lessons are many, and they are not superficial lessons. They are lessons that usually involve the heart. It does little good to think about a problem. One must feel the problem, for it is in the feeling that the heart will resolve it.

Now lastly we come to the Winter Season, for those who God refers to as the Winter People. This book is about the Winter People. These are the most severe lessons for the soul. It requires perseverance, a warrior aspect. Psychologists use the term *fight or flight*. The Winter People take a stand and they fight. They are deeply into truth. Their feelings are strong and complex and oh, there is so much love.

Readers, know that as you traverse these seasons on a soul level, that each one is honing you to become more brilliant with each lifetime, more caring, more compassionate, the ability to love at a deeper level. When one looks at one's fellow women and men and if you will look at the way the person handles the tragedies, the conflicts, the lessons in its life, it really is an open book for you. You will know if that soul is in the Spring Season or if that soul is in the Fall Season, or if that soul is in the Summer Season or *oh, that is a Winter Soul.* The Winter People are not difficult to point out. There will be something about them that will draw you to them. They are not stoic, but the peace they carry is palpable. They are not ferocious, but their fearlessness can be dramatic. They may not be that demonstrative, but their caring and love runs deep.

Readers, as you look at your neighbor with caring and discernment, non-judgment, know that that soul has a plan, has an agenda. You might call it a *contract.* For while the agenda may look like the person is not doing much, maybe that is what the contract entails—*now stay out of trouble this time,* their angel-guide maybe whispers to them with love. *Remember your contract; you are to watch and learn* (chuckles).

I Am Jeshua ben Joseph. I come to you this morning with my love, that at whatever stage or season you are in, dear readers, you are greatly loved—greatly.

Namaste.

Verling (Chako) Priest, Ph.D.—Scribe.

All right dear one, a little different. We will see what God does with this chapter, God's Children. *My love to you; have fun in transcribing!*

Thank you so much, Jeshua. There is no way I could have made all that up (chuckles). *Thank you so much.*

You are welcome, my dearest heart; over and out.

02-19-15.

ACKNOWLEDGMENTS

I wish to thank again the 10 participants who so willingly shared their death experience and introduction to Heaven. Each one's unique description adds richness to the book. I appreciate so much their humor, as well as their trust in me.

I thank Lord Sananda, the 11th subject, for his forthright description of his death story. And for his selection of the unique Entities who preceded him for the book—each depicting a certain category, those that did not yet realize they had died, and so forth.

My deepest gratitude and thanks to Celestial Blue Star and David of Arcturus for bolstering my channeling abilities when I started to waver with the last chapter. It was so controversial that I was thrown a little off balance. They guided me through it all, validating and suggesting a few changes in wording here and there to convey accuracy.

And last, but never least, I give my heartfelt thanks to dear Heather Clarke who has this nit-picking job of finding all of my typos and excesses (or lack) of commas. I would be lost without her expertise!

Therefore, my deepest gratitude and love to all…

LIST OF PREVIOUS BOOKS

Verling CHAKO Priest, Ph.D.
The Ultimate Experience, the Many Paths to God series:
BOOKS 1, 2, & 3 REVISITED (2011)
ISBN # 978-1-4269-7664-3 (sc)
ISBN# 978-1-4269-7665-0 (e-book)
REALITIES of the CRUCIFIXION (2006)
ISBN # 1-978-4669-2148-1
MESSAGES from the HEAVENLY HOSTS (2007)
ISBN # 1-4251-2550-6
YOUR SPACE BROTHERS and SISTERS GREET
YOU! (2008) ISBN # 978-1-4251-6302-0
TEACHINGS of the MASTERS of LIGHT (2008)
ISBN # 978-1-4251-8573-2
PAULUS of TARSUS (2010)
ISBN # 978-1-4669-209-1 (sc)
ISBN # 978-1-4669-2090-3 (e-book)
THE GODDESS RETURNS to EARTH (2010)
ISBN # 978-1-4269-3563-3
ISBN # 978-1-4269-3564-0 (e-book)
JESUS: MY BELOVED CONNECTION TO
HUMANITY AND THE SEA Revised Edition (2013)
CO-AUTHOR REV. CYNTHIA WILLIAMS
ISBN # 978-1-4669-7641-2(sc)
ISBN # 978-1-4669-7642-9(hc)

ISBN # 978-1-4669-7640-5(e)
MASTERS' TALES of NOW (2013)
ISBN #978-1-4907-1351-9 (sc)
ISBN #978-4907-1350-2 (hc)

ISBN #978-1-4907-1352-6 (e-book)
RELATIONSHIPS (2014)
ISBN #978-1-4907-5188-7 (sc)
#978 1 4907-5190-0 (hc)
#978-1-4907-5189-4 (e)

TRANSITIONS (2015)
ISBN # Pending.

Available at Trafford: 1-888-232-4444
Or, Amazon.com
www.godumentary.com/chako.

READERS' NOTES

ABOUT THE AUTHOR

Verling (CHAKO) Priest, PhD was born in Juneau, Alaska, hence her name of Cheechako, shortened to just Chako by her mother, a medical doctor, and her father, an Orthodontist. Chako was raised in Napa, CA. She attended the University of California at Berkeley where she met her future husband. Upon their marriage and after his training as a Navy pilot, they settled into the military way of life. They lived twelve years outside of the United States Mainland in various places, which included Hawaii, Viet Nam, Australia, and Greece. Little did she know that these exotic lands and peoples were preparing her for her spiritual awakening years hence?

After her husband's retirement from the Navy, they resettled in Napa, California. It was during this time that she returned to school at Berkeley, transferred to Sonoma University where she earned her first two degrees in Psychology. Chako then entered the doctoral program at the Institute of Transpersonal Psychology (ITP), renamed Sufi University, which is now located in Palo Alto, CA. She successfully completed that program which consisted of a Master, as well as the Doctorate in Transpersonal Psychology. Ten years and four degrees later she was able to pursue her passion for Metaphysical and New Age Thought—her introduction into the realm of the Spiritual Hierarchy and the Ascended Lords and Masters.

In 1988, Dr. Priest moved to Minnetonka, Minnesota. She co-authored a program called, *Second Time Around* for those with recurring cancer for Methodist Hospital. She, as a volunteer, also facilitated a grief group for Pathways of Minneapolis, and had a private practice.

She studied with a spiritual group in Minnetonka led by Donna Taylor and the Teacher, a group of 5 highly developed entities trance-channeled by Donna. The group traveled extensively all over the world working with the energy grids of the planet and regaining parts of their energies that were still in sacred areas waiting to be reclaimed by them, the owners. They climbed in and out of the pyramids in Egypt, tromped through the Amazon forest in Venezuela, rode camels at Sinai, and climbed the Mountain. Hiked the paths at Qumran, trod the ancient roadways in Petra, Jordan, and walked where the Master Yeshua/Jesus walked in Israel.

The time came, November 1999, when Chako was guided to move to Arizona—her next period of growth. This is where she found her beloved Masters, who in reality had always been with her. They were **all** ready for her next phase, bringing into the physical many books—mind-provoking books, telepathically received by her, from these highly evolved, beautiful, loving Beings. Each book stretches her capabilities, as well as her belief systems. Nevertheless, it is a challenge she gladly embraces.

It is now April, 03, 2015. She has finished writing her thirteenth book, *TRANSITIONS: Death Processes & Beyond of 11 Entities.* Blessings!

Comments to azchako@aol.com

Godumentary.com/chako

Printed in the United States
By Bookmasters